FACING

THE FINAL MYSTERY

FACING
THE FINAL MYSTERY

A Guide to Discussing
End-of-Life Issues

Second Edition

by

Laura Larsen, RN

BLUE SKY PRESS • MALIBU, CALIFORNIA • 2004

© 2000, 2004 by Laura Larsen. All rights reserved.

No part of this book may be reproduced, stored in a retrieval system, or
transmitted by any means, electronic, mechanical, photocopying,
recording, or otherwise, without written permission from the author.

First edition, 2002   Second edition, 2004

10 9 8 7 6 5 4 3 2

Printed in the United States of America

ISBN: 0-9746896-0-2
Library of Congress Control Number: 200309980

1. End-of-life 2. Death and dying 3. Spiritual concerns
4. Self-help 5. Communication

This book is printed on acid free paper.
Includes bibliographies and index.

Design: The Blue One

Published by
The Blue Sky Press
P.O. Box 6192
Malibu, CA 90264

To my Parents

Lois Driskell Larsen,
who taught me to "see it like it is!"

and

John Johannes Larsen,
who taught me grace and acceptance

CONTENTS

PREFACE

Facing the Final Mystery has been out in the world for more than a year. When people actually sit down and read the book, do the work, and report back to me, the comments are truly heartwarming. The feedback motivated me to continue this passionate project of encouraging all of us to face life by facing death.

Before printing the third batch of books, I decided to take the opportunity to remove the typos (and hopefully not create new ones), sparkle up the typeface and spacing for easier reading, update the resource contact information, and add the chapter on grief. I also wanted to find a less expensive way to print the book so I could offer group discounts to those who already expect them, such as organizations and institutions, but also to individuals forged into groups by the fire of necessity or by the heat of common sense.

The chapter on grief had to wait for this edition because up to this past year I thought it was something that came later, in a different book, after the mystery had been faced and death had occurred. Through continued "living and dying" experiences, I realized that bereavement, grief, and mourning may be present, in varying degrees, throughout our lives. I hope the additional information and resources will help the reader prepare for any state of loss.

Regarding the word final in the book's title, some friends and colleagues have pointed out that a physical death is hardly final. There is also work to do for those left behind, from making a memorial party, cleaning out closets, and mourning the loss, to creating a new way of life. There may be an afterlife to consider for the person who died. But "final" still fits my intention. It encompasses all areas of this life now that will arrive then, and that together are so difficult for so many to face. Besides, I like the alliteration of Facing the Final Mystery!

Malibu, California
November, 2003

PREFACE TO THE FIRST EDITION

In 1968, three years after I graduated from nursing school, my husband's nineteen-year-old sister, Carole, was brought into the medical clinic where I worked. A large truck had crashed into the rear of the Volkswagen bug in which she was a passenger in the back seat. Carole looked as if she were asleep; there was no sign of injury or blood. I automatically shouted for the doctor on call and grabbed a blood pressure cuff, while another nurse tended Carole's stepsister, Karen, the other passenger in the car. We had routines for emergencies.

The doctor lifted Carole's eyelids and examined her eyes. He immediately told me that her prognosis was poor and her internal head injury was so severe that her pupils were not reacting at all. He said he would initiate measures to try to keep her alive, but I must be prepared to lose her. The other staff members surrounded me and pulled me out of the emergency room into the doctor's office. I was eight months pregnant and they kindly wanted to protect me from personal trauma. I curled into a ball and wailed until I heard the arrival of the clinic's director, my boss. Surely he would figure out how to save her. As I emerged from his office, I saw the ambulance attendants carrying Carole's stretcher into the examining room where we placed dead bodies until the mortuary came for them. I did not go to her. I never saw her again.

In nursing school I had learned the medical tasks of death, including placing a paper shroud on a corpse and tagging its toe for identification. I was taught to close the doors of all the patients' rooms between that of the dead person and the elevator in order that other patients and their families would not see the covered gurney pass by on its journey to the morgue in the basement of the hospital. But I had not yet learned of the importance of experiencing the death of someone close to me and its shock of sudden loss and helplessness. Although the personal shock may always be unavoidable, I felt sadly unprepared for that day and the events that followed.

Not only was the day of Carole's accident horrible, but the next week was filled with both chaos and a kind of dullness. To reduce stress, my boss prescribed tranquilizers for Carole's mother and uncle; my husband chose canned martinis. Carole's divorced parents hadn't spoken for years unless they had to. This made communication awkward between family members and also prevented us from including both sides at the lunch after the funeral. I didn't know any of the rituals concerning funerals and forgot to invite my own parents. A kind man who knew nothing about Carole, her family, or her life, conducted the service at Forest Lawn. At least my mother-in-law told me I should invite people back to my home and prepare food for them. We sat indoors on a sunny day in my tacky mountain cottage. No one talked about Carole or told stories about her life and her spirit. It was a dismal affair.

During the ensuing weeks, tension grew inside me from unexpressed grief. I began to feel that we all should have known more about how to help each other through this enormous time of loss. I visited Carole's stepsister, whose boyfriend had been driving the VW. She happened to be in the same hospital where I was to give birth to my first child a few weeks later. We did not mention that Carole had died in the accident and only talked about the injuries Karen had received and her own prognosis. Coincidentally, in the same week I also visited a thirty-eight-year-old patient from our clinic who was dying from cancer. When she told me she was gaining weight because her malignancy was growing, I responded that I, too, was gaining weight because I was about to deliver. I still feel like screaming inside when I think of my insensitivity to that lovely woman who was reaching out to me, her family nurse, to talk about her illness and her approaching death. How had it happened that I did not learn from just living or being in nursing school to be able to listen and respond to her need to talk about this enormous transition?

The event of Carole's death was put aside except for my occasional visits with her mother when the two of us would reminisce. The other family members never initiated conversation about Carole, and when I did I felt I was disturbing their level of comfort, to say the least. Thirty years passed before Carole's father called me on the anniversary of her death to say he realized it must have been a difficult day for me, too.

I didn't know it then, but the seeds had been planted for my own exploration of the importance of confronting and discussing dying and death. Nine years later, in 1977, I heard Elisabeth Kübler-Ross speak for the first time at a holistic health conference in San Diego, California. Those dormant seeds began to sprout.

Elisabeth Kübler-Ross is the well-known Swiss psychiatrist who brought attention to the importance of facing and embracing dying and death. Her intensely moving stories and her outspoken, yet comfortable, way of telling them affected me deeply. As a nurse I had seen many people die, but I had never felt the feelings she described. I had never appreciated death as a transformation that is as important as birth. I had certainly not known of Kübler-Ross' concept that it is an honor to be with someone who is dying. Since destiny had allowed me to be the only family member present at the time of Carole's death, I regretted that I had not known to hold her and talk with her as she made that transition.

But Kübler-Ross was not the only powerful speaker at that conference in 1977. The leading proponents of alternative healing at that time, with their descriptions of the spiritual, emotional, and physical components of good health, also inspired me. My western medical curriculum had focused on disease and had not included the concept that we might be able to make choices promoting good health. Over the next two decades I read, studied, practiced and, eventually, taught Yoga, dance-exercise, massage, creative expression, and seeking one's purpose and mission in life. Along with many Americans, I believed we might live longer and better lives with these practices.

As my own middle age approached, I became aware that while death is inevitable, talking about it is discouraged in our culture. Then, three experiences stimulated my study of end-of-life issues in America.

First was my aging mother's incessant talking about her own impending death. Initially, I felt repelled and tried to change the subject. Nevertheless, as time passed, I became more comfortable and could stay focused on her needs. She was deeply afraid she would die a lingering and painful death. She asked me to help "bump her off" if she became incapacitated. Though our conversations decreased my sensitivity and repulsion to her ideas, I was pretty sure I couldn't help her end her life. I wondered what the alternatives were, and I began reading books and articles to see if I could learn how to ease my mother's fear of the dying process.

Second, a number of my friends' parents became seriously ill and some died. One had been living in a nursing home for four years following a stroke that left her paralyzed and unable to care for herself. An additional stroke caused her heart to stop beating; she was revived by a doctor who ignored her Do Not Resuscitate order. Another parent had created advance directives saying he wanted no life extension measures taken; but when he approached his death, he begged for anything to be done to save him. I knew three ladies in their late eighties who were each told they must have open-heart surgery or they would die. One recovered from the surgery, but continued to live the same life of loneliness, arthritic pain, and sleepless nights that she had endured before the surgery. The second also recovered from the surgery, but had a stroke six months later and lived for several years with twenty-four-hour care and without apparent awareness of her surroundings. The third initially chose not to have the surgery, but felt so weak she went ahead with it, suffered a stroke on the operating table, and was placed on a ventilator to keep her breathing. Meetings with the ethics committee were required to help determine when or if to remove the life support. I learned from each of these families that no conversations had taken place regarding the women's fears, the serious decisions that they were asked to make, and what the outcomes of those decisions might be.

Third, I watched a young friend undergo long and very painful cancer treatments, despite a very poor initial prognosis. She died at home with hospice care. Fortunately, I was able to witness my first, beautiful, at-home dying and death. Unfortunately, she had hospice care for only five days even though it was available to her months before. I began to see the possibility of a better way to die, and I also wanted to find out why beneficial care came so late to her.

I continued reading many excellent books on end-of-life issues. Each provided tremendous information, stimulation, and great value to me. Almost every one of those books contained at least one sentence that said some version of "If this had been discussed earlier, the trauma could have been less, disaster might not have occurred, and peace could have been made." None had discussed these potential conversations as a primary concern.

Gradually, the idea developed to write a book that would encourage conversations and dialogues about dying and death before a crisis occurred, as well as providing information and resources that would help us prepare ahead of time for our inevitable deaths.

As this book began to take shape, it became apparent that increasing the comfort with which we talk about dying and death is step one. Toward this end, I developed workshops that focus on exploring and expressing feelings, and practicing conversations about end-of-life issues. The willingness of people to talk about dying and death when encouraged to do so in a safe place further convinced me of the need to expand this concept. It became clear that when people can share these stories with each other, they feel relieved of emotions that had been stored and are often motivated to make changes in their lives. A surprising outcome during the workshops is that I hear just as much laughter as I see tears when the participants open their hearts.

Step two becomes initiating the discussions with the people we care about, once we remove the barriers that keep us from talking. These conversations can focus on the practical steps we want to take to prepare for our own death, but more importantly they can include and lead to deeper connections with our loved ones.

The major effect of exploring the feelings and having the conversations is that life becomes more real and immediate. The idea of putting off dreams until tomorrow takes on a new meaning. Seminal thoughts and ideas of the distant future brighten and call for expression now.

The initial force that moved me into this project was the hope that we might be able to prevent painful and fearful dying processes for our parents. Unfortunately, the habits, beliefs, and pride are often too set in our elders to allow the needed changes. This, combined with decreased memory capacity and hearing loss, can make conversations and new solutions difficult to initiate. I now feel it is more likely that the middle-aged, the boomers, and those younger will benefit and that we will also be able to help our children deal with our aging and dying.

However, it is not too late to try talking with our elders, and it is very timely to begin the conversations with our children and our peers. As I have read books, listened to people talk, and participated in workshops and conferences on dying and death, I see repeatedly that embracing death as a natural part of life definitely enhances the life we are living. I hope that you, too, will see why as you face the final mystery.

ACKNOWLEDGEMENTS

I wish to thank the following participants who brought this project into existence, thought by thought and page by page:

All of the families who willingly shared their stories with me, especially when deep feelings of loss, grief, and, sometimes, anger were still palpable.

All of the authors of the informative and inspiring books contained in the bibliography.

My friends who read the manuscript in its earliest form and then encouraged me to continue: Bette Albracht, Gale Gerhardt, Hedwin Naimark, and Barbara Bloch Villaseñor.

The brave and willing friends who each read the 200-page manuscript and filled them with post-its, red ink and pages of recommendations, knowing our friendships would continue anyway: Bette Albracht; Janet Bailey, RN; Dona Bigelow; Nita Carlton; Brigitte Englahner, RN; Carole Evans, RN; Erik Gillberg; Elissa Kline Gillberg; David Guelich; Carolyn Han; Melinda Johnson; Mary Ann La Vasseur; Lois Lyons; Pam Miller; Hedwin Naimark, PhD; Ruthann Saphier; and Jack Zimmerman, PhD. And

x

to Ann Berger, who read it fresh and encouraged me to complete the details.

Barbara Cameron for helping update my database.

All of the attendees of Facing the Final Mystery workshops, from 1997 to 2003, who shared their feelings so openly and helped each other explore their individual mysteries. They also wrote the poems that appear at the end of each chapter.

My cousin Marjorie Muns for being the artist that she is and for creating the beautifully depicted designs for each chapter with such grace and alacrity, including a new design for the new chapter.

Katherine Brown-Saltzman, who reconnected me to the nurses and other caregivers at the Circle of Caring Retreats and the Ethics of Caring Conferences, both sponsored by UCLA.

Julia Cameron for her book, *The Artist's Way*, which helped clear my mind and sort all of the concepts that began to flood my awareness.

Toastmasters International for growing my confidence, my ability to speak in public, and for providing the forum to compose and give speeches and receive feedback. Some of these speeches became the basis for the earliest chapters in this book.

Sonia Choquette for her audiotapes, *Creating Your Hearts Desire*, which helped me to focus my ideas and to believe I actually could write a book.

My weekly focus group, Diane Sanson and Kriss Smylie, who kept me on track.

My friend and astrologer, Tara Kamath, who with the stars supported my belief in the project.

All of the lovely people attending my dance exercise class, which kept my "computered" shoulders and back moving.

My adorable blueberry ibook computer and its matching Epson printer.

The many who sent articles and notified me of events, places and people, including most of the readers, and especially Maurine Doerken and Brigitte Englahner.

Special thanks to my son Erik Gillberg for listening,

supporting, and creating my website, lauralarsen.com. To Erik and his wife Elissa Kline-Gillberg for creating the cover of the first edition. And to my son Swen Gillberg for sitting with me as my father died. (And to all of them for incarnating as my sons and daughter-in-law.)

Very special thanks to my husband, Ron Galbavy, for teaching me about words, phrases, sentences and much, much more; for constant listening, support, and ideas; for reading and re-reading the manuscript; and especially for showing up.

Readers of the Second Edition manuscript include Carin Elin, Tara Kamath, Diana Meisler, and Lee Sorenson—Thank you!

Gracious input for the new chapter, "Good Grief," from Fredda Wasserman, director of adult services at Our House; Lothar Delgado, bereavement coordinator at Kaiser Los Angeles Hospice; and Marge Lewi-Rucker, group leader at Conejo Valley Hospice.

Designer-artist extraordinaire, Susan Dworski, for the brochure that got the First Edition out into the world, and for the Second Edition: cleaner, easier to read, and more beautiful.

To all of the many people who supported the First Edition and spread the word. You know who you are!

INTRODUCTION

Many traumatic stories were told to me early in this project. The traumas to families were physical, emotional, mental and spiritual in nature. They included invasive surgeries, painful treatments, and technical prolongation of life despite advanced illness or age. Families or their significant caregivers were "on hold" for months and even years, because they didn't know what their loved ones wanted or needed in relationship to their illnesses and treatments. Patients were often clinging to the last shreds of their lives because they were afraid of the dying process and what might occur after death. Financial havoc was evident in households, in extended families, in the way insurance companies would pay or not, and in the country as a whole as it wrestled with the national health-care crisis. While it seemed the problems were occurring near the end of life, as my study progressed I could see the causes of the problems had existed much earlier. Whether it was a month, a year, or a decade before, important, and often simple, conversations had not taken place.

The baby boomers—now in their early fifties—had not heard from their parents, nor told their children about hoped for end-of-life goals. A patient had not expressed his or her desires to a physician about the kinds of interventions desired or not. A physician had not described what a surgery or the recuperation period had really entailed. Family members who had become estranged had not reconciled with each other before death stepped in, and were experiencing guilt and longing for what might have been. Above all, the idea that dying and death was inevitable and an important part of living had become excluded from the conscious fabric of our lives.

I saw wise parents prepare themselves for the birth of their children and study each stage of growth and development. Birthdays, graduations, bar mitzvahs, weddings and more births were celebrated. Funerals were endured. Children were often excluded from attending funerals. I learned that many people had reached middle and old age without ever seeing a dead body, unless it was on television. If we don't see, hear, feel and otherwise sense death, how will we remember to talk about it?

The first draft of this book was filled with horror stories, such as those mentioned above. I thought I could scare the reader into embracing dying and death: "Look what can happen to you if you don't talk with your family now!"

I also believed that filling out the advance directives (documents that allow us to describe our end-of-life wishes and name an agent to speak for us if we cannot) could solve many of the problems that had occurred in the stories. The information would be written down. When a crisis occurred, a loved one would have access to that specific information. In fact, on many occasions when I began to describe this book or the workshops I was presenting, people responded by saying they had already "taken care" of that—facing dying and death—because they had created the documents. I still feel it is very useful to make advance directives, wills, and trusts, as long as the important or necessary people know where to find them. However, I now believe it is the conversations that explore the reasons, philosophy, and beliefs behind the choices, that hold the greatest value.

As my own journey continued, the avoidance of dying and death seemed especially curious to me when everyone I met who had personally "sat with death"—that is, they had actively participated in the dying process of a loved one—had been profoundly and positively affected. These people said their lives would never be the same again and they no longer felt afraid of their own deaths. Was this further evidence that our relegation of the dying to hospitals and the care of strangers was what had separated us from our final experience of life?

The final mystery is not that we will die. That is now more certain than taxes, given loopholes and deferments. The mystery is when we will die, what will happen after we die, and, most importantly, how we will die. Will it be sudden or slow, early or late, painful or peaceful? In this new century we must also consider our own effects on the mystery. Does technology provide a loophole to avoid death, or just a deferment? When is it a positive benefit to take a deferment? When does a technological deferment take us past the point of a peaceful death?

These questions and mysteries can only be addressed if we open our hearts and minds to the inevitability of death, to the possibility of increasing life's joy and intensity by participating in that awareness, and the willingness to talk with each other now.

THE PURPOSE OF THIS GUIDE

★ To explore the importance of and reasons for having conversations about dying and death now, before a medical crisis, old age, natural disaster, or political attack occurs.

★ To provide knowledge and resources to help you, your family, friends, patients, doctors or clients have these conversations.

★ To practice having the conversations with each other and our larger communities so that we may help change the climate of our culture regarding the denial, separation, and fear of death.

★ To have the conversations lead to improved end-of-life caregiving, decreased costs of medical care, and increased inner peace.

★ To infuse our days with the mystery of life by embracing death, now.

WHO SHOULD READ THIS GUIDE?

Facing the Final Mystery will benefit health professionals, people of all ages, and those of any faith or no faith. Reading it will help the middle-aged tend their parents and help prepare their children. Therapists can assist their clients, and nurses and doctors can help their patients, plan for end-of-life issues. Hopefully, it will help those interested in facing their own mortality have conversations with those who appear to be uninterested or afraid. So, everyone can benefit from reading this guide!

THE FORMAT OF THE GUIDE

Part I
Brief background and history of the denial of death in America. How we can continue to develop the pioneering work of Dr. Elisabeth Kübler-Ross, the hospice movement, and many writers, thinkers and caregivers who have explored dying and death during the last quarter of the twentieth century. Exploring the benefits and blessings of facing the final mystery now can help us begin, or continue, this journey with curiosity and enthusiasm rather than fear, dread, and denial.

Part II
Information, points of view, and personal experiences to help us begin to

ask questions about technological innovations, practical end-of-life tasks, and spiritual beliefs. Each chapter is designed to lead us to resources and provide new contexts with which to initiate conversations with our loved ones.

Part III

Integrating the information and points of view includes exercises, new ways to communicate, and how to bring these changes into our families and communities. We can begin putting the history, reactions, responses, and knowledge into action.

Part IV

Resources, including books, websites, and organizations to help you learn about the many options and opportunities for facing the final mystery.

USING THE GUIDE

* ★ For those of hearty mind or spirit, read it straight through to learn what areas you need and want to pursue further.
* ★ For specific problems or issues, read the appropriate pages indicated in the table of contents or index.
* ★ For ways to talk more easily with your loved ones use the exercises and action steps presented in Part III: Putting Facts and Feelings into Action.
* ★ For further education use the categorically listed resources.
* ★ Most importantly, enjoy it and share it!

In ancient cultures the word for hello and good-bye is the same. They understood something we are still learning— that arriving and leaving, living and dying, are two parts of the same thing…the One.

Susan Dworski, *The Invisible Vazimba*

PART I

The Death of "Natural Causes" in the 20th Century

Background and history of the denial of death in America and the benefits and blessings of bringing death back to life.

One

Where Did Death Go?

Learn how to live and you'll know how to die;
Learn how to die, and you'll know how to live.

—— Morrie Schwartz, *Letting Go: Morrie's Reflections on Living While Dying*

NATURAL CAUSES

What exactly were the "natural causes" of death that once were listed in obituaries? Surely our ancestors experienced most of the same ailments we know of today. Also in the past cardiovascular disease led to strokes and heart attacks; infection and hypertension caused kidneys to fail; cancer cells developed in all areas of the body they inhabit today; diabetes led to the same consequences of vascular insufficiency. The greatest difference in causes of death now is the decrease of infectious diseases resulting from the discovery of antibiotics. In fact, antibiotics have created the potential for many more of us to die of those "natural causes" by allowing us to live long enough for them to develop. Yet today, the cause of death is described by the medical ailment, or series of ailments, that immediately preceded it. Does this imply that death is "unnatural?"

Perhaps what had been considered to be "natural" was that the body was allowed to succumb to the failure of its systems, the encroachment of tumors upon vital functions, or the simple wearing out of organs over time. Also, people once died in the familiar surroundings of home, with loved ones, a family doctor, and often a personal clergy member present.

"Natural" may also have meant that death was expected, and thereby more accepted in the rhythms of the life cycle. The tragedies, as today, were deaths by tornado, fire, and flood, deaths too early of children and young parents, accidents, whether by horse and buggy, plane, or car, as well as the casualties of war. The many circumstances surrounding sudden deaths that no one could prepare for are what still feel most "unnatural."

DYING AND DEATH IN HOSPITALS AND NURSING HOMES

In America, 70-80% of all deaths now take place in sterile-feeling, unfamiliar and noisy hospitals or nursing homes. One reason for this is that dying may be accompanied by heroic medical interventions. Many of these measures are related to recently developed technical procedures, machinery, surgeries, and medications that require professional administration and maintenance. Another reason is that family members have moved away from each other, making care at home often unavailable. There is often little time or encouragement to move toward a "natural" death.

Medical technology has created the opportunity not only to save lives but also to extend life, often when there is no prospect of recovery. Pacemakers, organ replacements, heart bypass surgery, and dialysis are but a few of the interventions commonly used in elderly and severely ill patients. Medications can keep the organs functioning while, at the same time, the muscles, bones, and brain are deteriorating. Chemotherapy and radiation can be used to gain a little more time for some cancer patients, but the quality of life during this period may be very poor due to side-effects.

The training of physicians is just beginning to include instruction in how to be with patients and their families at the time of death. In addition, insurance costs, liability, and the need to use technology in caregiving have all but removed house calls. Once the caregiving has been relegated to medical professionals, families lose touch with the process of dying and the control over many of these options.

Young people are removed from this important time of life, as many hospitals will not allow children under a certain age to visit their ill family members. The lack of exposure to death has taken with it the conversations about death. When we don't see, hear, and smell the end of life, we also stop talking about it.

WHY WE DON'T TALK ABOUT DYING AND DEATH

In their book, *Death: A New Perspective on the Phenomena of Disease and Dying,* Manu Kothari, MD, and Lopa Mehta, MD, assert that much of the avoidance of discussions on dying and death has been largely perpetuated by the medical establishment through its focus on disease, its prevention, and cure. This makes dying a "failure" rather than an inevitable and normal life transition. If we are always moving towards "cure" through the next treatment, medication, or surgery, death does imply failure.

Yet, if doctors and technology created this situation, most of us in developed countries have absorbed and furthered these beliefs. We put our lives in the hands of doctors, abdicating our responsibilities by giving up our active participation in decisions related to dying. We willingly follow what the doctor says to do, often without question. When we do seek a "second opinion," it is usually from another doctor and seldom from our gut feelings, other patients' experiences, or our own research.

A GUILT TRIP

Another complication has arisen from an unspoken belief of the "New Age" movement: "I have caused my illness; therefore, I can cure it." While assuming that sharing some involvement in the cause of an illness may be beneficial in processing one's condition, to take full responsibility for it can only hinder that process in the same way that the medical establishment has by working only toward a cure. This point of view also leads us down the same path to "failure" should death occur. The guilt surrounding this kind of thinking leads neither to a cure nor to an easy death.

Furthermore, there are many conditions over which we have no control that contribute to illness and death. Some obvious factors include our genetic make-up, physical or emotional abuse, environmental toxins, available diet, and harsh climates. So, while it usually benefits us to take good care of our bodies in order to enjoy and extend our lives, we shall die anyway and at an unpredictable time.

FEAR AND DENIAL

Fear is often the underlying cause of not talking about dying and death. Will it be painful? Will I be alone? Will it be messy or undignified? What happens after death? Will I be aware of it or not? Will I go to heaven or hell, or maybe worse, to nowhere? What will become of the "I" that I think of as myself when I die? And will I feel I have lived my life to the fullest?

In his Pulitzer Prize-winning book, *The Denial of Death,* Ernest Becker states: "The idea of death, the fear of it, haunts the human animal like nothing else; it is a mainspring of human activity—activity designed largely to avoid the fatality of death—to overcome it by denying in some way that it is the final destiny for man." Becker links the fear of death to all heroic activities initiated by man. Exploring how denial of death relates to war, greed, and power may lead to a greater balance between our fears and our actions.

Over a century ago, Leo Tolstoy wrote a short story that illustrated the damage caused by denial. In *The Death of Ivan Ilych*, the protagonist watches with shock and outrage as his family and friends respond insensitively to his diagnosis, debilitation, and the approach of death:

> *What tormented Ivan Ilych the most was the deception, the lie, which for some reason they all accepted, that he was not dying but was simply ill, and that he only need keep quiet and undergo a treatment and then something very good would result. This deception tortured him—not their wishing to admit what they all knew and what he knew, but wanting to lie to him concerning his terrible condition, and wishing and forcing him to participate in that deception.*

He knew that he was missing the kind of caring he could receive, including pity, if they would accept the fact that he was dying.

THE PROBLEM WHEN WE DON'T TALK

Why is not talking about dying and death a problem since we will all live and die with or without talking about it? It is true that talking about dying and death will not change its inevitability. It may not decrease the pain and disruption to our lives. But it is highly likely that not talking about this second most important transition of life— the first being birth—and the only transition that every one of us makes once we are here, may lead to some combination of the following situations:

★   Fear and anxiety remain unabated by not learning about potential solutions for pain, treatment, caregiving, and existential concerns.

★   Unspoken financial and practical wishes cause confusion and upheaval in our families.

★   Poor medical choices are made due to lack of information and can lead to increased pain and prolonged dying.

★   Increased costs to our families and our health care system occur because we value the length of life over the quality of life.

★   Not planning ahead for the extensive kinds of caregiving needed in the future leads to chaos when the crisis occurs.

★   Rifts in close relationships are left unhealed because we believe we can "do it later."

★   Dreams and visions remain unfulfilled because we believe we have more time.

★   Enormous gaps in our communication with loved ones develop because we skirt around the unavoidable processes of living and dying.

We not only need to learn the language of living and dying but also develop the courage to speak it.

Death finds fresh lives

Glowing, growing, groping

Grabs ahold, takes vital roots

Death stays, holds, waits

Gnawing, needing, knowing

Hands touch, reach, plead, relax

H.F.

Two

Death Begins Its
Journey Back to Life

The only incontrovertible fact of my work is the importance of life.
—— Elisabeth Kübler-Ross, *The Wheel of Life*

BIRTH WENT INTO THE CLOSET
AND CAME OUT AGAIN

Death isn't the only life event that deserted the home. Looking at the way birthing went to the hospital and came home again can illuminate the changes now being made with end-of-life care.

With the advent of hospital births, complete anesthesia for delivery pain, and the development and convenience of formula feeding, the birthing process also became separated from life at home. Birthing, like dying, became a medical procedure, rather than the natural beginning of a lifetime. An expectant mother could go to the hospital at the first sign of labor. She often remained in the hospital for up to two weeks, with the baby sleeping in the nursery and being fed formula by nurses. Emotional bonding between parents and the child was not considered important, nor was the constant touch we now know to be so valuable in nurturing a baby to full physical and emotional health.

Yet, by the 1960s, many people began realizing this picture was not good. Robert A. Bradley, MD, Ferdinand Lamaze, MD, and Frederick Leboyer, MD, among others, began teaching awareness during pregnancy and birth to both parents; midwives again became involved in healthy births; fathers were allowed to be present and, frequently, other family members as well. A new concept was born— the birthing room—combining the best of both worlds: a homey setting with loved ones present, music, a variety of postures allowed for the actual birth, and nearby medical equipment and professional expertise for potential problems. The nursing of babies resumed its "natural" place in life, and circumcision decisions were reconsidered.

DYING IS ALSO A NATURAL PROCESS

Like birth, death can also blend the best values and practices of the old and the new. Time-honored experiences of families sitting at the bedside of dying loved ones can be combined with skilled hospice caregivers, who may also provide technical equipment and medication to soothe and relieve pain. These arenas will be discussed in depth later in this book and are mentioned here because of the similarity to the birthing rooms.

In the same way that couples attend birthing classes to prepare themselves for the event of birth, we can be learning ahead of time what to expect from the dying process and death itself. Our lives are marked by many transitions throughout the years. The final passage is just as powerful and valuable as the first one, perhaps more so, since it is our life's culmination. Then, once we reduce our fears and acquire a realistic sense of and participation in these wondrous and universal processes, we may embrace and celebrate them both.

THE DYING AND DEATH MOVEMENT

In the last quarter of the twentieth century, a movement began to make death a part of life, largely spurred on by the groundbreaking work of Dr. Elisabeth Kübler-Ross. As a psychiatrist, she encouraged doctors to talk openly and honestly with their dying patients. She went on to write many books, including *On Death and Dying* (1969) and *Death: the Final Stage of Growth* (1975), and to give lectures around the country. Her stages of dying—denial, anger, bargaining, depression and acceptance—became a model for end-of-life studies. They provided a language to examine death and the need to provide more humane and honest treatment for the dying.

The publication in 1974 of Raymond Moody's book, *Life After Life,* brought the concept of "near-death-experience (NDE)" into public awareness. The shared experiences—of the bright light often at the end of a long tunnel and family members waiting to greet them—brought peace to those who had gone through such transitions. Many people who had previously been afraid to discuss what had happened to them now felt comfortable to tell their stories. In addition, while corroborating Moody's conclusions, many of these people described how their lives changed dramatically, often with illumination of their purpose in life. More collections of such stories were published, and the door opened to the possibility of peace and reunion after death of the physical body.

The hospice movement emigrated from England to America by way of Dame Cicely Saunders. Hospice care began here at a grass-roots level, with volunteers providing care to the dying. By the end of the twentieth century, professional hospice organizations proliferated throughout all our major cities and even small communities; they provided both medical assistance and volunteer services. Availability and knowledge of hospice services have grown, while Medicare and most health-care plans provide financial reimbursement when it is needed.

The AIDS epidemic and increasing cancer-related deaths brought the topic of death, especially at a young age, to greater public awareness. Support groups for these and other illnesses began opening the doors to talking about dying and death. Movies, books, marches, walks, and fund-raisers showed the willingness of people to continue the support for exploring and learning how we can respond to life-threatening illness and to death in new ways. However, most of us don't participate in or move towards these activities and discussions until we are personally touched by a serious diagnosis or other severe emergency.

Because medical technology provided the means to extend lives, sometimes beyond the wishes of the patient, advance directives were created. These forms allow the patient to write down—in advance—his wishes regarding end-of-life care, with various options. The patient may request all measures be used to save life, only specific measures in certain situations, or none at all. There is still a great need to educate the public about how to create these documents and where to locate them during a crisis.

In addition, there is an increasing interest and curiosity about Eastern thought concerning death and afterdeath states. This is especially true of Buddhist ideas and practices, which have long encouraged and taught the importance of preparing for death. Spiritual teachers, including the Dalai Lama, Stephen Levine, Ram Dass, and Joan Halifax have brought new kinds of help to the bedsides of the dying. They have also created organizations and centers to teach people how to be with others during the dying process.

During the 1990s, philanthropist George Soros created an organization called *Project on Death in America,* through which grants were made available to those who were promoting, teaching, or administering better end-of-life care. Hundreds of thousands of dollars were given to individuals, schools, and organizations working on many different aspects of end-of-life care.

In 1997, a simple and touching story was told of a wise man, dying from a chronic, debilitating disease. Morrie Schwartz' former student, Mitch Albom, chronicled his weekly visits in the book *Tuesdays with Morrie.* During the last months of his life, Morrie increasingly lost control of his abilities to care for himself. Yet, he remained alert and determined to observe, understand, and most importantly to feel the changes as he was living them. In the intervening years, a television documentary and movie further disseminated this kind and thoughtful man's observations about life, love, dying, death, and the importance of loving relationships.

In early 2000, journalist Bill Moyers announced his plans to present a televised series called *On Our Own Terms: Moyers on Dying in America.* Along with the development of the series, Moyers and his colleagues created a network of interested individuals and organizations around the country to promote awareness of and the need for better end-of-life care. By the time the TV series was aired in September of 2000, hundreds of town meetings had taken place across the country to examine the local needs for end-of-life care. All those who participated are now able to meet and connect, via email and the Internet, to continue learning from one another as better ways of care are developed and put into practice.

Yet, with all this extensive and intimate exposure to aging, dying, and death, what are we doing with the wisdom we have been given? How are we incorporating these lessons into our own lives? When will we begin facing our own final mysteries?

IT IS NOW TIME TO INCORPORATE THE
DEATH AND DYING MOVEMENT INTO DAILY LIFE

The groundwork has been laid. The information is accessible. It is time to take advantage of what others have experienced so we know where to turn for help and how to find information and guidance *before* a medical crisis occurs. It is now time to learn and remember that death is a vital part of life. We can do this by beginning the conversations now.

Dogwood begins to bloom

White against the black forest

Promising beauty.

D.B.

Three

The Benefits and the Blessings

*The expectation that we can be immersed in suffering and loss daily
and not be touched by it is as unrealistic as expecting to be able to walk
through water without getting wet. This sort of denial is no small matter.
The way we deal with loss shapes our capacity to be present to life more than
anything else does. The way we protect ourselves from loss may be
the way in which we distance ourselves from life.*

—— Rachel Naomi Remen, *Kitchen Table Wisdom*

WHY BOTHER?

As we saw in the last chapter, death left our households in America
in the twentieth century, and some active and compassionate people
and organizations have been working hard to bring it back. But
why? What is wrong with sending the sick and the dying to
someone else at some place else for care? After all, we are busy these
days and we don't have the skills to manage the technology needed
for care. And talking about the end of life is morbid, isn't it? Decay
smells. Death brings loss. It spoils a good evening to bring up such
topics.

So what if our children fight or fret over our belongings? We'll be gone then and they can work it out. And if we have to agonize over a parent being kept alive or allowed to die because we didn't know their wishes, time passing will heal this wound, or at least lessen its impact. And besides, don't the doctors know best what to do about these decisions?

THE DARK AND THE LIGHT

But what are we throwing out with the bath water surrounding dying and death?

Donald says he doesn't want to discuss dying and death now because they are going to happen later anyway; why talk about this painful and scary subject twice? Meanwhile, Donald feels depressed. He has been retired for ten years, but has never figured out what he wants to do with his days. He is anxious when his wife goes out of his sight, and he follows her around the house and yard as she does her tasks. Is there a connection?

Consider a common situation: If we feel anger towards a friend and do not express it or discuss the possible cause of it, that anger can fester or grow. This may result in an explosive interchange with the friend, or even be foisted onto an innocent bystander (witness road rage or kicking the dog) in a degree much larger than the original incident that caused the angry feelings. The unexplored anger may also prevent positive and necessary communication or affection from taking place.

Ignoring the fact that we will die may create a similar situation. Living as if death only happens to other people, or at least only when one is really old, separates us from the fibers of life. It is as if the weaving of our days has only the main threads that go up and down and left and right. There is no color, no texture, no design, no pattern. Remembering that we die and actively weaving that memory into the fabric of our lives enhances the quality and richness with which we make our daily choices regarding work, love, charity, creative expression, entertainment, and having fun.

If the subject of dying or death does arise in conversation, it is often related to wills, trusts, or advance directives. A typical response might be "Oh, we've had our attorney draw those things up," or "I'm going to take care of those documents soon," as if this is the only kind of participation needed. While the creation of these documents may provide benefits for all involved, the blessings will come from the deep levels of feeling, connection, and understanding derived from facing the final mystery.

ASK THESE QUESTIONS:

★   By learning about and discussing the medical technology that allows us to live past the healthy functioning of our organs, can we begin to take better care of our bodies at an earlier age?

★   By examining our personal belongings and savings, can we not only prepare our finances for our heirs but also become more conscious of how we earn, spend, save, and give now?

★   By telling our families how we wish our funerals or memorials to be conducted, can we also place greater value on the rituals and passages that we celebrate throughout our lives?

★   By imagining what our loved ones might say about us at our memorial *parties*—not just memorial "services" or "ceremonies"—can we begin living our lives in a way that might be worthy of personal and professional accolades or celebration?

★   As we learn the kinds of questions that people ask as they near death about the needs for settling issues with loved ones, can we take better care to communicate and express our love to family and friends now?

★   By considering the end-of-life issues now, can we

develop a greater focus on the meaning, purpose, and spiritual aspects of our lives as we live them?

As we prepare ahead of time and learn to accept that we will age, become ill, and die, either suddenly or over time, there is a great likelihood that we can bring greater clarity and vibrancy to each day. We may begin by examining the *quality of life* that we want to enjoy now, as well as exploring the conditions under which we do not want to live. We can imagine how much pain, depression, or stagnancy we may be willing to endure, while appreciating the unpredictable feelings that will probably accompany such states. We can reach now for joy, energy, awareness, passion, enthusiasm, and movement.

SITTING WITH ILLNESS AND DYING

Although many roads may lead us to a deeper comprehension of life's meaning relative to illness, dying, and death, two pathways stand out. The first path involves facing our own mortality if we should personally become diagnosed with a life-threatening disease, as well as the critical brushes with illness and death of those we love.

The second road is exposing ourselves to those who have lived to tell their stories, and those who have made a lifework of dying and death. Reading any of the following books contributes to the knowledge, light, and power needed to live through our own situations.

PURPLE HAIR AND A WARM HEART

Dr. Elisabeth Kübler-Ross has combined her decades of experience with those of David Kessler in their book, *Life Lessons*. Each chapter describes a particular lesson learned during the care of dying patients, as well as Dr. Kübler-Ross' own experiences since her stroke in 1995. In one story, she describes a woman who felt great concern for her son, who had purple hair, numerous piercings and always wore the same dirty T-shirt. The mother said she nagged him constantly and that she could never say a nice word to him. After attending a seminar with Kübler-Ross she was struck by the possibility that her son could die at any moment, in which case she would live the rest of her life remembering that her revulsion to his attire was the subject of their last conversation. She came home from the seminar, embraced her son, wearing the same dirty T-shirt, and told him she loved him just as he was. She saw him as a young man, a boy, her son, a person striving to be someone, instead of the composite of his adornments.

BELOW AND ABOVE

Dr. Jean Shinoda Bolen uses mythology as a backdrop to illustrate the opportunities that may arise from the crisis of severe illness and approaching death. In her book, *Close to the Bone: Life-Threatening Illness and the Search for Meaning*, Dr. Bolen explores how we may heal the soul by descending into the underworld. The ancient stories help us to see that no matter how painful the impending loss and change are, we have options as to how we will respond. If we include humor and develop a fresh perspective on our suffering, we may have a very different journey than if we either give up or fight blindly to survive.

FROM VITRIOL TO MUSIC

The novelist Paulo Coelho tells of an interesting experiment and treatment of a young woman who has failed at her attempted suicide. In *Veronika Decides to Die,* we watch Veronika's healing toward life through her interactions with other patients in a mental institution, the influence of belief, and the sound of music. Her doctor is exploring the concept of vitriol, the quality of being bitter or caustic, as a cause of despair. The relationships between routine, conformity, and madness are intertwined with poetry, music, and choice. Impending death illuminates the value of life for her.

LIFE BEFORE DEATH?

Two Buddhist writers guide us to the connection between living and dying. The first, Larry Rosenberg invites us to focus on the question "Is there life *before* death?" in his book, *Living in the Light of Death: On the Art of Being Truly Alive.* The author describes the messengers of Aging, Illness, and Death that the Buddha encountered when he ventured into the real world and then encourages the reader to contemplate the reflections of change and impermanence to make our lives more precious.

The second writer, Stephen Levine presents a year-long program to reclaim our lives in, *A Year to Live: How to Live this Year as If it Were Your Last.* From working for decades with the dying, Mr. Levine noticed the regrets and remorse that people express if they have the opportunity. They are sorry to have neglected spiritual growth, to have avoided joy, to have worked too long and too hard, to not have explored specific interests or knowledge, or to have stayed too long in difficult relationships. Using these (and other) findings, the author guides the reader to consider and use these concepts in a journey of self exploration so that when the last moment does come, it doesn't seem like it is too soon.

HOSPICE HEALERS

In each of the books listed in the annotated bibliography under PALLIATIVE CARE AND HOSPICE, skilled caregivers tell us of the enlightenment, the unfolding of the mystery, and the joy we can experience if we are prepared to die, and the sorrow, pain, and clinging to life if we are not.

THE BENEFITS AND THE BLESSINGS

The rewards for facing the final mystery now may be practical or physical (the benefits), or emotional and spiritual (the blessings).

THE BENEFITS

*   We may decrease physical pain and the fear of the possible pain of our "final illness" by learning sooner, rather than later, about pain management and palliative care.
*   We may decrease the cost of our "final illness" by learning more about the possible outcomes of medical choices, such as statistics on rates of cure, degree of pain and side effects, or length of time predicted for treatment.
*   We can decrease anxiety by thoughtfully considering our practical end-of-life wishes now, so our survivors won't have to guess and argue over such things as what ceremony or method of body disposal we desire.
*   We can reduce or prevent discord by preparing wills and trusts now that will enable our survivors to honor our wishes. Conversations ahead of time about our financial choices for dispersing our assets or estate will help even more. Will-reading surprises can cause upheaval when children were not warned ahead of time what they might expect.
*   We can make better decisions about the medical choices that may face us by learning how to ask better questions and gather more knowledge.
*   We can enjoy better health, increase our work options, develop new skills, and change our daily routines when we face the final mystery now.
*   Perhaps best of all, we can help our loved ones do the same for their lives.

THE BLESSINGS

★   We can bring heightened awareness to our lives as we live them. By facing our fear of death and accepting its natural inevitability, we can feel more deeply connected to life now, embracing all that it offers. Food tastes better. Leaves appear greener. Flowers are brighter. Laughter is deeper in the belly. Procrastination may disappear when we remember that "waiting until later" may never occur.

★   We can begin now to widen our experiences, fulfill our dreams, and remember our purpose in life as we honor that we may not be able to do so later.

★   We can improve our relationships with those we love by realizing that now is the best time to work things out. Or, by acknowledging that there may be those who will not work things out with us, we can let the situation go and stop the struggle.

★   We may help our loved ones have a more peaceful dying process by learning to accept death and, when the time comes, to let go of our loved ones and our own lives.

★   We may enjoy some amusement as we lighten up a topic that has been relegated to hushed whispers.

BEGIN THE JOURNEY NOW

When we face the final mystery, benefits and blessings will befall us as surely as aging, illness and death. Let us begin the journey by exploring our feelings and talking with our loved ones, now.

When all petals drop

Do we lose the one we love?

Flower is still there.

D.B.

PART II

Transforming Perspectives:
Facing the Final Mystery
in the 21st Century

*Information, points of view, and personal experiences to help reduce
the fears that keep us from having valuable conversations
about end-of-life issues.*

Four

Many Maps for the Journey

Facing the dread of the future is an excellent vehicle for entering into the spiritual dimension. We must be willing to open to all that the moment contains, including that which seems most threatening. But how do we do this? By cultivating fearlessness and familiarizing ourselves with our demons.

— Ram Dass, *Still Here: Embracing Aging, Changing, and Dying*

WHAT WE ARE NOT CONNECTED TO, WE FEAR

It is likely that the greatest impediment to facing the final mystery is fear. Fear wears many masks. There is fear of both the dying process and fear of what comes after death. Fear keeps us from learning what may be of help to us when we near the end of life. Fear prevents us from having the conversations in which we can help one another make preparations for this important transition.

The following quotation by Edmundo Barbosa in Sukie Miller's book, *After Death,* provides a philosophical opening and perspective on the flesh and bones struggle with dying. He says:

...the [first] benefit to the dying person of stepping fully into the truth: strife ends when truth prevails; one need no longer struggle. To resist truth is pain; to accept it is to enter seamlessly into reality. Many people suppress the knowledge of impending death out of fear of dying in the here-and-now and fear of harsh judgment and punishment after death. But with truth comes the knowledge that the pain is in the resistance, [emphasis added] not in the truth.

The second benefit is riskier to explain, for there is as far as I know no scientific confirmation of it. But my long experience with the dying has convinced me that denial increases the agony of death and, conversely, acceptance—readiness, or ripeness, and embracing the truth—brings ease.

In this chapter, we look at a few of the many ways people have confronted dying and death from spiritual, emotional, religious, and psychological points of view. By reading about the cultures of other people and times, the concepts of those who have explored these issues in depth, and the experiences of those approaching death's door, we may help open our hearts and minds to possibilities and opportunities that otherwise might have escaped us.

DEATH AS TRANSFORMATION

What if we, Americans living in the twenty-first century, could shift our perception of death from being a failure to death being a reward and celebration?

In *The Denial of Death,* Ernest Becker quotes the anthropologist A.M. Hocart as saying, "Primitives were not bothered by the fear of death...that death was, more often than not, accompanied by rejoicing and festivities; that death seemed to be an occasion for celebration rather than fear." Primitives celebrated death, he says, because "they believed that death was the ultimate promotion, the final ritual elevation to a higher form of life, to the enjoyment of eternity in some form."

Becker goes on to say that "most Westerners have trouble believing this any more, which is what makes the fear of death so prominent a part of our psychological make-up." Yet, even in contemporary cultures, some people do embrace death as a reward instead of a punishment.

CELEBRATING IN BALI

Roberta and Mark were visiting Bali as tourists. One day they were walking along a road when a procession approached them. Children and elders were dressed in beautifully colored clothes, carrying food and flowers, and making lively music with percussion instruments. A young woman called out to them, "Come! Our grandfather is dead! We are going to celebrate!"

Mark and Roberta proceeded with them to an area near the graveyard. The grandfather's body, carried on a bamboo stretcher, was placed in the center of a clearing. The family first undressed him and then began bathing him. All participated, even Roberta and Mark. The mothers allowed their children to spread soapy water on Grandfather's body. It was considered both an honor and a joy to touch the dead body. There was no sense of it being a "corpse," or that the procedure was unclean.

The old gentleman, now dressed in his best clothes, was placed in a box filled with beautiful offerings, important tools he had used, and food and other items he might need for his journey. Then he was carried uphill to the graveyard and lowered into a hand-dug grave. Family and friends placed more flowers and offerings around him. Next, everyone took turns scooping dirt into the grave with cupped hands. Everyone cheered and clapped when Roberta and

Mark did the same. The younger men finished the job with shovels, while the family returned to the clearing to celebrate with food and music.

Roberta felt uplifted by the villagers' joy and reverence toward both the grandfather and death itself; she knew she would never feel the same about this cycle of life again. Indeed, later, when her father and a good friend endured long, difficult dying processes, Roberta was able to face the challenge gracefully and calmly, assisting and comforting the dying loved ones. Then, she was able to guide other family members to do the same.

LIVING A FRUITFUL LIFE

Henri Nouwen is a highly regarded Catholic priest, teacher, and prolific writer, who talks about dying and caring for the dying in his book, *Our Greatest Gift*. While living and working in a community that cared for mentally challenged people, he watched the caregivers and the residents help each other through every stage of living and dying. Over time he discovered a simple truth: by acknowledging and remembering that we all die, we remember *we are the same*—on the same path. In fact, in a paradoxical about-face, it is *being alive* that separates us from one another and causes loneliness. Embracing death can begin the journey to wholeness because we realize we are like everyone else.

Nouwen discusses the difference between *accomplishing* (doing) and *being fruitful* (being). In fact, he suggests, our fruitfulness becomes more apparent after we have died, while our accomplishments are only important while we are alive. He says:

> *The real question before our death, then, is not, How much can I still accomplish, or How much influence can I still exert? but How can I live so that I can continue to be fruitful when I am no longer here among my family and friends? That question shifts our attention from doing to*

being. Our doing brings success, but our being bears fruit.
The great paradox of our lives is that we are often concerned
about what we do or still can do, but we are most likely to
be remembered for who we were.

BUDDHIST PERSPECTIVES ON DYING AND DEATH

A basic tenet of Buddhism is that we cannot truly live until we have fully embraced death, that if we are not prepared to die, we cannot be prepared to live.

Soygal Rinpoche, a noted Tibetan Buddhist teacher, was asked by a student what he hoped to accomplish with the publication of his book, *The Tibetan Book of Living and Dying.* He replied, "I want every human being not to be afraid of death, or of life; I want every human being to die at peace, surrounded by the wisest, clearest, and most tender care, and to find the ultimate happiness that can only come from an understanding of the nature of mind and of reality."

His book is considered to be one of the most complete presentations of Buddhist teachings ever written and can be used by everyone. Included are practices to be applied during the dying process and rituals to help the soul through the processes of the afterdeath.

A second perspective of Buddhist thought comes from Christine Longaker, whose husband died of leukemia in his mid-twenties. The deep grief she suffered led her in two directions: creating and working in the Hospice of Santa Cruz County, in California, and studying Tibetan Buddhism with Soygal Rinpoche. For the past twenty years, she has devoted herself to helping others make this transition in life, at the bedside of the dying, and teaching others how to learn from these experiences. Her book, *Facing Death and Finding Hope,* amplifies and interprets the Tibetan principles, making them accessible to non-Buddhists.

She condenses and explains the "four tasks" of living and dying:

★   Understanding and transforming suffering
★   Making a connection, healing relationships, and letting go
★   Preparing spiritually for death
★   Finding meaning in life

Applying these principles enriches every aspect of daily life, as well as helping us prepare for death.

NEAR-DEATH EXPERIENCES

While there is much controversy over the actuality of near-death experiences (NDEs) in the scientific community, there have been reports of such phenomena throughout history. As early as the eighth century, the historian Bede records the story of a man returning to life, after being considered dead for the night, to tell of his miraculous experience of traveling toward great light and being met by a guide.

There have also been such accounts in the writings of Plato, Tolstoy, and Carl Jung, among others. In the 1970s, books were published by both Elisabeth Kübler-Ross, MD, and Raymond Moody, MD, that described people's stories of returning to life after being resuscitated from an accident, heart attack, or other serious illness. While each story had variations, most contained some combination of the following properties:

★   A sense of peace
★   A rushing sound as they separated from the body
★   The ability to look down upon the scene they had left and overhear conversations about themselves
★   Darkness leading to light, often through a tunnel or cave
★   Extreme natural beauty
★   Visions of relatives who had preceded them into death
★   Some kind of life review

The most important aspects reported by almost everyone who had an NDE are the strong needs to live their lives in a completely new way, to do good for others, to follow their dreams, and to release the fear of death.

Many in the scientific and medical community have offered explanations for these experiences ranging from lack of oxygen, to change in body chemistry, to temperature variations, or they maintain the stories were fictitious. They insist the people have not truly died.

Even if clinical death does not occur, these stories awaken curiosity and pose questions to our rational certainties. Those who have had a near-death experience undergo some kind of spiritual or psychological transformation. It is as if they had prepared for death during the event. In a few minutes or hours, they seem to have accomplished what many take years to study within a disciplined spiritual practice.

TRAVELING LIGHT

At the age of sixty, Rex walked outside his house and collapsed from a massive heart attack. A neighbor saw him fall and called 911. Rex reports that he not only hovered above the scene of the paramedics reviving him, he also witnessed the neighbors praying for him. In addition, he traveled to another state where he could see his brother preparing for a fishing trip. Rex was able to recount the details of conversations, the number of paramedics present, and the specific neighbors who were gathered in prayer.

When he recovered, he changed his life work from being a comfortably retired accountant to becoming a thanatologist—one who studies and teaches about death. His experience was so poignant and powerful that, in

association with a hospice organization, he began counseling
patients who were dying and their families in how to remove
their fear of death.

WHEN IS A GHOST NOT A GHOST?

From an early age, psychotherapist Carla Wills–Brandon was drawn
to the stories of people who experienced phenomena while present
with a dying loved one. At the moment of her mother's death in a
distant hospital Wills–Brandon, who was then 16, was awakened at
home and knew her mother was gone. Her mother's two sisters were
awakened at the same moment and also knew.

In addition to her own experiences, Wills–Brandon compiled
stories from the lives of friends, patients, as well as some from books
published early in the last century. Her book, *One Last Hug Before I
Go: The Mystery and Meaning of Deathbed Visions*, describes the various
kinds of visions—what people see, hear, smell and feel—that
occurred at or near death. These include a dying person who begins
to chat with someone in the room who others cannot see, a
caregiver who sees or feels the presence of someone near the person
who is dying, and warnings of impending death in the form of a
dream. What the visions have in common is the *peace* they bring to
the loved ones who witness them.

Brandon published this book to help people understand the
universality of these visions, as well as to encourage us to consider
the possible meanings and options that they present, such as life after
death and benevolent assistance at the time of the passage.

FOLLOWING DEATH, WHAT?

Another interested seeker has focused specifically on what various
peoples think happens after we die. Dr. Sukie Miller, author of *After
Death: How People Around the World Map the Journey*, was exposed to
death as a child through her father's home medical practice. She

became curious about "what happens next." As a psychotherapist specializing in patients with terminal illness, she learned that dying people came to her for comfort and relief of anxiety, but often they did not want to look at what might happen "next." She began to "wonder what other cultures, those more comfortable with the idea of death and freer about asking such questions, could teach us about the value of consciously contemplating the afterdeath."

Dr. Miller learned that most cultures and religions share some form of four distinct stages: *Waiting, Judgment, Possibilities, and Return.*

Waiting is where "rest is possible, fear abates, and the traveler prepares for the trip." Relief comes next through *Judgment*, wherein the spirit is "liberated from uncertainty, ambiguity, and the suspense of waiting...the future is determined and the traveler is propelled forward on its journey." The third stage, *Possibilities*, reveals potential goals of the journey. These include everything from heaven and hell, angels, light, time, space and the revelation of purpose. Finally, most cultures include some form of *Return*, whether it is reincarnation or resurrection. She observes that "Implied in the leaving is the return; contained in death is the seed of rebirth."

AFTERDEATH INVENTORY

As Dr. Miller began to set up her Institute for the Study of the Afterdeath, she met and interviewed experts who worked with dying patients to gather their experiences. One psychiatrist in particular admitted she never asked her patients where they thought they were going after death, because she just didn't have the words to ask the questions. Dr. Miller then created the "Afterdeath Inventory," which can be found in her book. These questions may be used not only by the dying person but also by family, friends, and professionals who assist in the dying process. Answering these questions, she says, can bring a clarity that leads to comfort and decreased fears.

One engaging application of these universal stages is how they play a continuous role in our lives while we are living. We are always waiting, in between stages. We are always *judging,* usually ourselves. We constantly seek *possibilities* for our next steps. And then we return to some part of ourselves, hopefully renewed, with more wisdom.

WHAT IF THERE IS NO AFTERLIFE?
WHAT IF THERE IS NO HIGHER PURPOSE?

How does one find purpose in life and face death without the thought of an afterlife, reincarnation, or higher guidance? One answer comes from the Humanist point of view, which encourages us to live each day fully, to do good for others, and to fulfill our purpose and goals. They promote this view because *this life* is likely to be the *only life,* and not because we fear that we will be judged—promoted or demoted, saved or damned—by an external power.

Albert Ellis, PhD, founder of the Institute for Rational Emotive Behavior Therapy, presents a stark, yet not uncommonly held, position. When asked by William Elliot, (as quoted in Elliot's book, *Tying Rocks to Clouds*) to describe his beliefs about life, Ellis responded, "The Universe is meaningless and there are no supernatural beings in the world. It is foolish to be afraid of being dead. Death is exactly the same state as before we were conceived: zero, nothing. We didn't exist at all then…therefore there is nothing to fear about death. We have only this one life, and therefore we'd better make our own meaning and enjoy ourselves as much as we can without needlessly harming other humans."

THE DEATH GREMLIN

In 1992 Gale Warner, a poet and journalist, was diagnosed with lymphoma at age thirty. She kept a daily journal for the next thirteen months, until her death, about the course of treatment, her poignant feelings regarding nature, friends, the support of her husband, and her passion to live.

A friend asked Gale what she believed happened after death. Gale responded, "I told her what had been 'transmitted' to me last July by the *death-gremlin*." The gremlin said to her:

> *Death truly is a mirror and reflection of life, the other half of the spinning wheel, the counterwhirl in the spiral dance. When we are on the other side, we are able to choose our way of being, just as we can in life. We can choose the steepness of our learning curves, decide how many risks we want to take, how much effort we want to expend. We continue the patterns and attitudes we have chosen in life, although the crisis and revelation of crossing the threshold gives us an opportunity for a sudden inspiration and a leap to a new level.*
>
> *Some people believe that dying means becoming unconscious or asleep, and that's probably what they will find. Some choose to let go of their separate self and relax into a universal oneness and harmony. Others fiercely retain their individual souls. Some even choose hell, believing that this is what they have earned. And some choose to become activist angels focusing much of their attention on helping those on this side, the side of life. There are myriad ways of being in death, just as there are of living life. After entering death, at first there is great euphoria, as mysteries and truths long forgotten are joyfully remembered and revealed, the relief of leaving the heaviness of the ill body becomes apparent, and we are welcomed with open arms. There is an initial time of blissful rest and relaxation, if we need it. Then come the choices, the opportunities—different than the ones we face in life, yet also similar. We 'live' on the other side, on the blue road of spirit. Existence on the other side contains sadness, but the predominant emotions of the other*

side are great joy and radiance, and blessedness, and the
primary activity is praise. Gradually, we feel a longing to
return to life. Perhaps we see there is something we must do,
a mission we must accomplish. Perhaps we simply find
ourselves longing for the smell of flowers, the taste of fresh
water, the joining and touch of bodies, the sound of laughter.
Perhaps we reach a point where we understand that in order
to continue to grow, we must step back into the counterflow
of the dance.

Gale Warner died a week after sharing this conversation with
a friend. Her husband then edited her journals into the book,
Dancing at the Edge of Life.

WORLD RELIGIONS AND DEATH

Kenneth Kramer is an Associate Professor of Religious Studies at
San Jose State University. In his book, *The Sacred Art of Dying,* he
describes how world religions understand death. By telling stories
and describing practices and rituals, he illustrates the attitudes toward
death of Hindu, Buddhist, Zen, Tibetan, Chinese, Mesopotamian,
Egyptian, Greek, Hebraic, Christian, Islamic and American Indian
traditions.

Kramer says, "Each of the religious traditions teaches, in one
way or another, that the best way to prepare for one's own death is
to anticipate the death experience while yet alive."

THE DOORS OF PERCEPTION

We know we can use medical technology for diagnosis, life-
extending procedures, and pain management, but it will not keep us
alive forever. Trying to reduce our fear of death with technological
"fixes" does not work. What will work is shifting our own
perceptions about what death means. Our inner attitudes can

provide the control we want once we see death as a natural and unavoidable consequence of being alive.

Daniel Callahan states in *The Troubled Dream of Life: In Search of a Peaceful Death,* "We do not readily talk about how to shape our interior life in the face of death, because we think its meaning to be private, not easily shared or explored with others. Yet of course death is a universal experience, and it derives its meaning as much from this universality as from the different circumstances of individual lives and deaths."

These, and the previous points of view, suggest and perhaps declare the hunger of the human heart to find an explanation or meaning for our lives. Discovery of our own conscious purpose and meaning becomes a much greater challenge if we haven't had some kind of explanation provided for us, or if the old foundations of perception, thought, or faith no longer support us. Yet, the opposite position finds us without a sure sense of footing on any ground. Maybe searching for our purpose and meaning becomes the purpose for living. Whatever our perspective, the only guarantee is that some one else will see it differently.

Opening wide our own doors of perception and being willing to shift our inner attitudes may allow the conversations to begin. The talking will bring us closer to one another and help us gain a sense of control over our destinies.

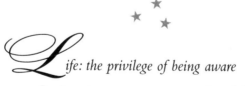

Life: the privilege of being aware
Is given to us so we can grow in wisdom
And, in departing, pass the privilege on to others

H. F.

Five

Palliative Care & Hospice

Through my years as a hospice doctor, I have learned that dying does not have to be agonizing. Physical suffering can always be alleviated. People need not die alone; many times the calm, caring presence of another can soothe a dying person's anguish. I think it is realistic to hope for a future in which nobody has to die alone and nobody has to die with his pain untreated.

—— Dr. Ira Byock, *Dying Well: The Prospect for Growth at the End of Life*

SUFFERING AND RELIEF

Palliative care and hospice provide the core of effective and humane end-of-life care. The purpose of discussing these care concepts is to enable the reader to understand the services they provide, the benefits to be gained, and the importance of learning about hospice *before* a terminal illness is diagnosed. The differences and similarities between palliative care and hospice will be defined, as well as where, when, what, and how these services are obtained.

Learning that it is not necessary to suffer physically during the dying process may reduce fear, allowing us to open our minds and hearts to the discussions that can benefit us at this time of our lives. It may also help us understand that *death with dignity* can be achieved through good care and that death "with a lot of tubes" and assisted suicide are not the only options.

WHAT IS PALLIATIVE CARE?

The National Hospice and Palliative Care Organization describes palliative care as "treatment that enhances comfort and improves the quality of the patient's life. No specific therapy is excluded from consideration. The test of palliative treatment in hospice care lies in the agreement by the patient, the physician, the family, and the hospice team that the expected outcome is relief from distressing symptoms, easing of pain, and enhancement of quality of life."

Palliative care and hospice are *the same* when the patient's illness is likely to be terminal and comfort care is needed. They *differ* when the patient has a good chance of recovering and comfort is provided until a cure takes place.

For example, any patient recovering from surgery, illness or accident will be given care to palliate their pain and discomfort as they heal. Or, palliative chemotherapy or radiation as an aspect of hospice care might be given when a cancerous tumor is growing in such a way that it is causing pressure on organs or nerves and surgery is not deemed possible. Relief of pressure can be obtained for a time even though the goal is not cure.

Medical pain management has improved dramatically with the development of new drugs and treatments. Also, the idea that too much pain medication can lead to addiction and should be avoided has been modified. Addiction is not likely to occur and it is certainly not an issue if the patient is near death. Almost all conditions can be successfully treated for pain and other distressing symptoms.

PAIN AS THE FIFTH VITAL SIGN

In addition to checking temperature, pulse, respiration and blood pressure, health-care providers are being taught to assess the level of pain as described by the patient. Zero is no pain. Ten is the worst we can imagine, not necessarily the worst we've ever had. A level of two or three might allow continuation of daily activities.

If the patient can converse, a series of questions can help assess the location and severity of the pain. An illustration of facial expressions may also be used with children or when verbal expression is not possible.

In addition to this measurement, awareness is also increasing among health care providers to encourage additional pain management techniques, such as massage, guided imagery, herbs, and acupuncture. If we, as patients or family members, are aware of ways to determine and treat pain, we can further the advancement of such ideas.

WHAT IS HOSPICE?

The National Hospice and Palliative Care Organization describes hospice as "A philosophy or program of care rather than a place; a unique blend of services that addresses the *physical, emotional,* and *spiritual* needs of the terminally ill person and his family. Hospice care is provided by an interdisciplinary team of professionals and volunteers, guided by the goals of an individual plan of care."

Dame Cicely Saunders developed the concept and practice of hospice, as we know it today, in England. The first hospice care organizations in the United States were established in the 1970s. While hospice has been available for almost thirty years, many people do not receive these excellent and unmatched benefits until the last few days of life.

The reasons for this are several, beginning with our society's resistance to discussing matters related to dying and death. In addition, both the patients and their families may be hesitant to seek hospice care, thinking it means giving up hope. There has not been sufficient education of the public as to the benefits of hospice by their doctors, health care organizations, or even by hospice itself. It is therefore very important that we learn everything possible about hospice care so that we understand how the dying process can be improved.

WHEN IS HOSPICE CARE AVAILABLE?

To receive payment from Medicare and other insurance coverage programs, a doctor must write a referral saying that the patient is not expected to live more than six months. Because this is an almost impossible prognosis to make, many people receive hospice care too late. The national average duration of hospice care in the United States is currently less than thirty days. The time to ask for hospice care is when the patient needs more care than is available from the family or the staff in a nursing home or hospital, and when pain is not being managed or comfort provided.

In addition to pain management, hospice team members assess the patient's needs and help procure equipment and treatments that can be beneficial months before death occurs. Therefore, it is extremely important to gather hospice information before diagnosis of a life-threatening illness to learn exactly when hospice care can begin with the best results.

It is important to understand that if a patient under hospice care gets well or goes into remission, hospice care can be terminated. On the other hand, if the patient continues living past a six-month period, hospice care will continue until no longer needed.

Hospice is available for patients of any age and any diagnosis. However, some insurance companies may not pay for traditional treatments once hospice care is initiated. If a patient decides to resume treatment to cure the disease, they can discontinue hospice and resume at a later date, if needed. These issues can be explored fully at the time hospice care begins.

There are also hospice organizations that are completely funded by donations and grants. In such cases, there is no need for a doctor's referral or requests for payment by insurance or Medicare. If a patient does not have insurance or if the diagnosis is unclear in terms of time, such an organization is ideal. It is very beneficial to visit the hospice organizations in your area to learn what kinds of services they offer.

ARTHUR: "I INTEND TO GET WELL."

Arthur received a serious diagnosis of metastatic bone cancer. He initiated spiritual counseling with a deep belief his illness would go away. I didn't want to challenge his belief and yet I could see how much he and his family could benefit by hospice care.

I presented it to him this way: "Arthur, I know you are working diligently to remove this disease from your body. But until you are better, hospice can keep you more comfortable, allowing you to be free from pain and thereby able to read and study more easily. If you no longer need their care, they'll stop visiting. They will also provide tremendous help to your wife so that she won't become exhausted looking after you."

Because he was experiencing pain and difficulty moving about and could already see the toll on his wife's wellbeing, he agreed. A hospital bed arrived at once. A date was made for the health-aide to help him with a shower each week. He remained pain-free, continued his spiritual studies, and was able to say good-bye as he approached death.

WHERE IS HOSPICE?

Hospice care may be given in a home, a hospital or nursing care facility, or in a special place designed for end-of-life care only. This could be a Hospice Inn, or a Dying Center. It is not the *location* that makes it hospice; it is the care and compassion administered wherever it best suits the dying person and his or her family.

About 80% of hospice care in America currently takes place at home. It is required that there be an able and willing caregiver living in the home, and who is available twenty-four hours a day. Family members act as the core caregiving unit with the hospice team members providing the professional support and knowledge, medical intervention, and link to all other useful services. If there is no family member available, there is the possibility of securing a volunteer or friend to become the main caregiver.

It is important to note that if the dying process continues over several months, a single, primary caregiver will need more help. If sleep deprivation or exhaustion sets in, the hospice may arrange for the patient to spend several days in a board-and-care facility to provide respite for the family member. Additional caregivers who can stay during the night may also need to be hired. Discussing these possible needs before a crisis may help determine what additional help can be gathered from the community.

There is a need to create more residential hospice centers to serve those dying patients who do not have family members available to help with home care. Some hospitals are now designing or designating hospice wings as the benefits of hospice care are becoming known.

There are a few hospices in the United States specializing in the care of dying children. Not every hospice is staffed with pediatric nurses.

HOW DO WE GET HOSPICE CARE?

The first step is for the patient's doctor to write a referral to the hospice organization. If the doctor does not suggest hospice care, the patient or the family must ask for it. If the doctor does not comply by writing a referral, the family can go straight to a hospice organization and have the hospice doctor make an assessment and referral or they may seek the opinion of any other doctor. If your doctor does not know the name of a hospice organization, you can locate one by asking friends who have used their services, call the National Hospice and Palliative Care Organization, or look in your local yellow pages. Medicare and most insurance companies now provide full coverage for hospice care, and the hospice nurse or social worker can help you establish relations with your insurance company.

WHAT ARE THE SERVICES PROVIDED BY HOSPICE?

Once the referral is made, the hospice organization will send a medical social worker and/or nurse to evaluate the situation in the home or the nursing home. It can usually be determined from this first visit, what kinds of care will be needed. Hospice can provide special equipment, including beds, wheelchairs, commodes, medication, and other medical supplies. Home health care aides help with daily activities and also teach family members needed skills. Additional care and visits are available twenty-four hours a day, as needed.

Most hospices depend on volunteers, who have been extensively trained, to help the families in many ways. They may read, talk, run errands, or sit with the patient to allow the family a respite. The companionship the volunteers provide becomes an important part of the hospice service.

In addition to meeting the physical needs of the patient and his or her family, hospice professionals provide tremendous emotional, psychological and spiritual support. A chaplain is available to discuss the spiritual needs. Support groups, usually led by a social worker, are provided for family and friends of the dying person. Bereavement counseling services are also offered, before and after death. The hospice support teams not only have training in all of the needed techniques and resources available, but also have the experience of having participated in the dying process of many, many patients.

WHY WE NEED TO LEARN ABOUT HOSPICE NOW.

Writing in the quarterly newsletter "Choices" for Fall, 1998, Naomi Naierman states, "Hospice as a concept suffers from a powerful denial syndrome in our society. Hospice must be better understood if it is to reach all that need it. When all Americans know what hospice is, they are more likely to make it an explicit part of their long-term plans, and their fear of death will be abated. Increased visibility of hospice locally and nationally will result in more people becoming active advocates for themselves and for their families."

Contacting hospice from the moment of diagnosis of any progressive, life-threatening illness should be the first step. It may not be necessary to hire hospice caregivers at that time, but their insight and experience can help families know what lies ahead. Hospice caregivers may be better able than doctors to assess when there is six months left to live.

ANNA

My first personal experience with hospice occurred when my friend Anna, age 37, came home from the hospital to die. She and her husband had been determined to "beat" her invasive cancer. However, the extra-strength chemotherapy and radiation did not provide the hoped-for results of recovery. Anna and her family agreed it was enough and called hospice service to prepare for her arrival at home.

A hospital bed was set up in the den where Anna could look out to her garden. The hospice nurses had set up an IV so that Anna could self-administer her pain medication as she needed it. All of the implements needed for her caregiving were provided.

When I arrived, I was asked to sit with Anna while the family went outside to receive counsel from the hospice social worker. They learned what her physical symptoms might be as the final changes began, how they could best assist her, and how they could help each other with their own grief. The hospice nurse had taught Anna's best friend Ginger how to add medication to the IV, giving her a useful task as she spent time with her dear friend.

For the next five days there was always someone sitting at Anna's side, holding her hand, ready to help adjust her position, give her ice chips, clean her mouth and just be with her.

The first day I sat with her she opened her eyes and with a big smile said, "Hi! What are you doing here?" I replied, "I'm sitting with you while your family is out in the garden learning how to help you stay comfortable." Anna grinned and said, "Well, bless your heart!" We squeezed hands and she began to doze. She was able to connect with each of her family and friends as we took turns being with her. Those big blue eyes, so willing to make clear contact with each loved one, contributed to the healing of everyone present.

Later that day I gave massages to Anna's mother and husband, long overdue for some personal respite. I took another turn of sitting with Anna during the night so they could sleep. Each moment seemed very precious. An intense connection with Anna and the greater sense of life unfolded in a way I had never known. Even my professional nursing career had not afforded this tender experience.

During the following days, the hospice nurse visited to make sure everyone had what they needed, answering questions, offering suggestions. She was the support to this loving family who wanted to do the best they could for Anna's passage.

The last night of her life, Anna opened her eyes to see her Mother at her side. "OK Mom—tell me what's gonna happen." "You mean where you'll be going?" "Yes, Mom." Her Mother quoted Bible scriptures that were familiar to them both. She told her they would be together again, and that Anna would never leave her heart. Anna smiled and closed her eyes. She stopped breathing peacefully at 4 a.m., with her husband at her side and both of her parents in the room.

Anna's mother and Ginger bathed her and dressed her in a beautiful gown, sprinkled rose petals across the bed and put soft music on the CD player. As the daylight grew, Anna's husband called the rest of the family and a few friends.

The hospice nurse came to pronounce Anna dead and to answer questions.

I felt privileged to be included that morning as we all sat around the bed, everyone sobbing, no one saying "Don't cry." Anna's mother occasionally prayed out loud. We even had humor. One of Anna's adoring brothers admitted that during the days of waiting, he had been reminded of the Monty Python movie where the guy, as he continues to lose body parts, keeps saying "I ain't dead yet!" The laughter from everyone released another chunk of stored emotions and was soon followed by more sobbing.

The emotional catharsis of this time continued the healing for all involved.

For me it was life changing. As a nurse I had been present at many deaths in hospitals, yet I had never experienced these deep connections among family members, *the emotional outpouring, and the involved participation in the dying process. It was a spiritual experience, instead of a medical one. I am grateful.*

Dr. Ira Byock says, "The ultimate responsibility for end-of-life care must remain with the dying person and the family." The more we can learn now by reading, asking others who have used hospice, and researching the availability connected to our own insurance policies and geography, the more likely we will reap the bountiful benefits in a timely fashion.

Find faith, fall free

Feel the fathomless fullness

No heavy heart.

See selfless support

Set someone's soul sailing

Silently surrendering

Back to beginnings,

Never ending

Joy.

J.M.

Six

Bioethics

*Ethics will probably be the single most important
issue of health care in the future.*

— Margaret Mahoney, PhD, RN, *Nursing Ethics Network*

THE ETHICS OF LIFE AND DEATH

The advent of medical technology created the need to discuss how
the technology is used. This discussion—the ethical consideration of
medical practice, health care delivery, and biologic research—is
called *Bioethics*. The scope of Bioethics includes beginning-of-life
issues, genetic research, resource allocation, (who gets what in terms
of care, organs, and procedures), and end-of-life bioethical dilemmas.
While these categories require distinct consideration, each one
ultimately affects the choices we need to make and the information
we must gather as we face death.

Dr. Jack Kevorkian has brought attention to the most well-
known bioethical issue in our country. He is the doctor who has
assisted terminally ill patients to commit suicide, even live on "60

Minutes." While people who are pain ridden and ill may consider him a benevolent solution to their predicament, many are repulsed by his aggressive tactics, less than comfortable surroundings for his death assistance, and flagrant violation of "normal" ethical considerations.

Whatever the response, "Dr. Death" as his detractors call him, has almost single-handedly alerted us to the concept of Bioethics. He has probably caused more conversations, formations of committees, reviews of legal ramifications, and plain public awareness than the ethics' scholars, doctors, and clergy combined. For this we can be grateful. From this public dialogue, we can begin to explore our own points of view and gather more information so we can converse with each other as we assess the life and death issues that have become complicated by technological interventions.

In addition, we can learn more about other possibilities for a peaceful and dignified death than Dr. Kevorkian's focus on assisted suicide.

THE IMPORTANCE OF DISCUSSING BIOETHICAL ISSUES NOW

Most hospitals now have ethics committees that help patients and families examine these problems when they arise, but their services are usually offered when a medical crisis is in full swing.

Before we find ourselves in an ethics committee meeting because a loved one needs either more care, less care, or no care, we can learn more about the ramifications of potential future decisions now. While it is likely that most of us will never need to discuss the cloning of sheep or genetic research, bioethical issues will touch almost all of us in one or more of the following ways:

    ★   ***Potential bioethical dilemmas*** occurring because we don't know the language and haven't written and shared our wishes

★   ***Physical and emotional impact*** to a loved one or ourselves because of the difficult process of decision making, or the outcome of such a decision

★   ***Financial impact*** to us directly due to a personal illness or that of a family member, and indirectly through increased cost of medical care, and insurance premiums

POTENTIAL BIOETHICAL DILEMMAS

Becoming familiar with some of the medical terms used in making bioethical choices helps us have needed conversations, both to make our decisions and to create our advance directives.

No-code decisions: Do not resuscitate (DNR)

If you've ever been in a hospital or watched "ER," you may have heard a blaring sound, followed by doctors and nurses running. This means a patient has been "coded," or that *code blue* has been initiated. This scene occurs when a patient's heart suddenly stops beating—medically called *cardiac arrest*. Code blue is the sound that alerts the resuscitation team in the hospital to move very quickly to try and save that patient's life. This special team likely includes an anesthesiologist, a respiratory therapist, and nurses and doctors trained in advanced cardiac life-support. The need for intervention is immediate. For a patient or family, code blue means there is no time to discuss options. This alone should encourage us to examine its implications now.

CPR means *cardiopulmonary resuscitation*. It is usually a combination of techniques to stimulate the heart to beat again by compression or medication and to force air into the lungs. CPR must be initiated at once. A "crash-cart" that contains all the needed equipment and medications is now positioned on every hospital floor.

There have been countless lives saved by CPR, such as when a child has fallen into a swimming pool or someone suddenly collapses. The bioethical dilemmas occur when the patient is either very ill or very old and the crisis—such as cardiac arrest—would have resulted in an old-fashioned natural death. Who makes the decision of whether CPR should be used or not? If we have not created and made available our own written requests, the ambulance driver or the emergency room physician most likely will make the choice. Until we educate ourselves, we won't even know what questions to ask. Until we consider the meaning of our lives, we won't know the answers.

The *no-code* instructions are described in the DNR. If the patient has signed a DNR and that document is available, she will not have a lifesaving intervention. A DNR may be filled out along with other advance directives, or when a person enters a nursing home. It will always be requested when a patient begins hospice care.

Stopping life-extending treatments once they have been started

A common scenario is that after emergency resuscitation a tube to facilitate breathing is inserted, or to get through a temporary inability to eat a feeding tube is inserted. If the patient gets well, these interventions are stopped. However, when the patient remains gravely ill or goes into a coma, the bioethical dilemma arises of how or when one should stop these treatments. If there is little or no chance for recovery, the dilemma escalates when the family knows the patient would not want to be maintained in such a way, but there are no written instructions from him.

The news-making bioethical stories most pertinent to our discussion here are those related to life extension technology.

NANCY CRUZAN AND HUGH FINN

In 1983, Nancy Cruzan, in her early twenties, was severely injured in an automobile accident. She was resuscitated and because she was unconscious, a feeding tube was permanently inserted into her stomach. After four years with no improvement of her condition, her family sought to have the feeding tube removed. The case ultimately was taken to the Supreme Court, "right-to-life" activists became involved, and another three years passed before the court *allowed* the tube to be removed. The final decision was based largely on the verbal testimony of her friends and family who had *heard* Nancy say she would not want to live under such circumstances. Had Nancy written her wishes on paper, she and her family would have been spared years of suffering.

More recently, Hugh Finn, a television anchor from Kentucky, was kept alive for three years by means of a feeding tube. His wife knew he would not want to be sustained, but there were no written instructions. His brother and his wife's sister believed he should not be allowed to die. Again, the court had to intervene. He died eight days after the tube was removed.

Is "pulling the plug" murder?

Such issues become even more difficult when the patient is a child. In one case, a ten-year-old girl died from a malignant brain tumor. Her lungs were still inhaling and exhaling by means of a ventilator. When the doctor in charge suggested to the parents it was time to "pull the plug," they refused saying their religion would consider that murder. The parents took their daughter home with the equipment still attached, and she lived another fourteen months. During that period

911 was called many times.

When is it time to cease treatment?

How can we determine when medical technology is not providing a cure but is only extending the days of a patient's life, maybe with increased pain and discomfort? Conversation about these moments ahead of time can at least provide a base from which to ask questions in order to make such decisions in the future.

Comprehending the available kinds of treatments, especially those that provide pain relief and increased comfort, allays fear and helps a patient and family to let go when there is no hope of cure. Knowledge of how hospice care works and how to receive it can make this period of time one of grace instead of terror.

Withholding of nutrition and fluids

When a patient is dying, she begins to lose her appetite and later her thirst. This is a natural and desirable progression toward death. Yet, the thought of withholding nourishment and allowing a loved one to "starve to death" seems appalling to many. Family members may feel guilty about agreeing to such a course. Physicians may fear lawsuits. It becomes a bioethical dilemma.

Once appetite and thirst have subsided, withholding nourishment does not increase discomfort and may allow someone who is seriously ill to let go. Learning this helps family members support the dying process. Having discussions ahead of time also helps the family members know they are acting in accord with the patient's wishes and eases such decisions. Coming to a collective agreement on such a course is the responsibility of all involved.

HELEN AND SCOTT NEARING

Helen Nearing describes the death of her husband of fifty years in her book, Loving and Leaving the Good Life. *"A month and a half before Scott went, a month before his hundredth birthday...he said: 'I think I won't eat any more.' He never took solid food again. He deliberately and purposefully chose the time and the way of his leaving. It was to be methodical and conscious. He would cast off his body by fasting. Death by fasting is not a violent form of suicide; it is a slow gentle diminution of energies, a peaceful way to leave, voluntarily. Externally and internally he was prepared."*

Helen fed Scott juices for a month and then he asked for water only. "He did not sicken. He was still lucid and spoke with me, but his body was extremely emaciated. The life force in him was lessening...slowly, gradually, he detached himself, breathing less and less, fainter and fainter; then he was off and free, like a dry leaf from the tree, floating down and away. 'All...right', he breathed, seeming to testify to the all-rightness of everything, and was gone."

Limiting treatment during dementia, vegetative state, or coma

In addition to food and water being withheld, if a patient reaches an irreversible vegetative state or advanced dementia other modes of treatment come into question. When is it time to discontinue medications and treatments that are prolonging life? Again, this is especially difficult if the patient has not written her wishes or had conversations with her family members and doctors.

For example, pneumonia was once called "an old man's friend." There may be a time when an elderly and ill person contracts pneumonia. *Not* treating him with antibiotics might be the way to allow a more peaceful death, as well as preventing death by a more painful cause. These are never easy decisions to make, especially for someone else.

We can all benefit from examining such situations before they occur, gathering as much information as is available and assessing our feelings about our own lives—how we determine when life still has meaning and purpose, or when we are just existing.

Assisted suicide and euthanasia

Euthanasia means that one person is helping another to die. It may be active when a medication is administered, or passive when a life-sustaining treatment is withheld or removed. When the patient is fully involved in this decision it is called *voluntary euthanasia*. If the patient has not requested assistance in dying from another person, it is called *involuntary euthanasia* and has sometimes been known as a *mercy killing. Involuntary euthanasia* can also be used immorally and should never be confused with active or passive euthanasia or assisted suicide.

Assisted suicide means one person is helping another to die with the dying person's consent and request, and is the same as voluntary euthanasia, either active or passive. *Physician-assisted suicide* means it is a doctor giving the help. The *right-to-death* and *death-with-dignity* movements have focused on making such an action by a doctor legal. Their adversaries are calling such actions murder.

As discussed earlier, the possibility and desire for assisted suicide to occur has created the most well known bioethical dilemma in our country. It has developed largely out of the fear that death will not be "dignified" and that one will end up in the hospital "full of tubes." Many consider suicide, assisted or not, as the only solution to this problem.

Following are points of view from people who have worked with patients who have requested such assistance.

Author M. Scott Peck, MD, discusses the spiritual and medical controversies regarding euthanasia and mortality in his book, *Denial of the Soul*. Through the stories of his many patients and his own reflections on life and death, he explores the relationship of life's emotional and physical pain, what can happen when that pain becomes too much, and the soul's journey through this process. He illuminates how "taking a life" differs from "allowing death," whose consent is required for euthanasia, when physical or emotional pain might become grounds for euthanasia, and what we can learn from the process of dying a "natural death." He emphasizes that if people learn there is improved pain relief available, they won't be as fearful of the dying process.

Another compassionate physician, Timothy E. Quill, MD, surprised the medical community when he published an article describing his own experience of helping a long-time patient with end-stage leukemia to die. He assisted her by prescribing barbiturates that he knew she would take when she felt the increased symptoms of her disease and the decrease in her sense of control. He expresses his sadness that she had to die alone in order to protect her family and her doctor from being accused of helping her to die.

Quill includes the above story in his book, *Death and Dignity: Making Choices and Taking Charge*. While he believes that modern pain relief will allow most people to die comfortably, he feels there are a few people who will have anguished deaths. He addresses the issues of choice, control, and fear that face a person with a terminal disease. He encourages creating advance directives before there is acute, serious illness resulting in potential loss of mental capacity.

Both of the above-mentioned books address the

enormous scope and breadth of deciding the *when* of death. They also address how difficult it is to define the line between choosing to die actively or to commit slow suicide by excessive use of nicotine, alcohol, or exposure to dangerous situations.

Almost as infamous as Jack Kevorkian, Derek Humphrey has championed the right for people to die when they choose. His journey has also been surrounded with controversy, including the assisted suicide of his first wife. His book, *Final Exit,* and his organization, the Hemlock Society—now called End-of-Life Choices—provide specific information about committing suicide without causing legal problems for the family. The main mode of exit is to take a certain number of barbiturates that a person has saved up himself from legal prescriptions. Tying a plastic bag over the head is the step to ensure completion of the task.

Discussing euthanasia and assisted suicide illustrates the differences between actively seeking death, allowing it to come at its own time, and not prolonging the dying process. The more we talk, the more we access our feelings. The more we talk, the more we learn about what is available in palliative care and the more tools we will have to consider end-of-life choices. Dr. Marion Primomo, a pioneer in hospice care states, "Almost all hospice patients who initially request suicide change their minds as soon as they feel cared for. Only one in 1,000 follows through."

The physical and emotional impact of bioethical decisions

Not knowing what kinds of care our loved ones want and not having considered our own beliefs and ideas regarding end-of-life interventions can lead to great upheaval on many levels.

MARGARITA: WHEN IS DEAD, DEAD?

Margarita was 80 and had been living with the assistance of thrice-weekly dialysis treatments. She continued to care for her longtime husband Benny, who had advanced Alzheimer's, as well as high blood pressure and arthritis. Despite these conditions, it was he who drove his beloved wife to her treatments, incurring numerous fender-benders though no serious accidents.

Then Benny died from a sudden stroke. Margarita continued to get herself to the treatments at her HMO for six more months and then awoke early one morning with chest pains. She pushed her LifeLine necklace, which had 911 programmed into it. She also called her neighbors, who arrived at once. As the neighbor held Margarita in her arms, Margarita clearly assessed and expressed calmly, "I am dying." She stopped breathing. And then the paramedics arrived. Because they were called, and it is their responsibility, they resuscitated her and took her in the ambulance to a nearby hospital (not her HMO). There, despite the fact that she had a flat brain wave, they connected her to a ventilator to keep her breathing. In the next four days she was dialyzed twice.

Margarita's niece Annie returned as quickly as possible from Arizona to find her aunt in this situation. Annie thought there was a Do Not Resuscitate order in Margarita's papers, yet no one had made an attempt to coordinate her care with her HMO. When she asked why these heroic measures had been taken, the doctor said it was felt that a slow or postponed death was easier for the family to embrace. (Margarita had no immediate family; Annie was her closest relative and would have advocated for the cessation of her treatment had she not been away.) With Annie's insistence, the machines were shut off and Margarita was pronounced dead.

Annie was left wondering if Margarita was in pain as she went through this. She also noted that the medical costs paid by Medicare were $85,000 for the four days of her extended life.

Financial impact of bioethical decisions

Keeping a loved one alive because technology is available does not necessarily mean it is in the best interest of the patient. The technology may also bankrupt the family financially or emotionally before this question is ever asked. Furthermore, these costs are transferred to all of us through increased insurance premiums and depletion of the entitlement programs, such as Medicare and Social Security.

According to the Medicare Current Beneficiary Survey of 1992-96, the last year of life expenses constituted 22% of all medical costs, 26% of Medicare (with 50% in the last two months), 25% of Medicaid, and 18% of all non-Medicare expenditures. While these figures have remained stable over the past two decades despite the increase of technology, they are quite significant in terms of health care dollars spent when death follows soon after. Furthermore, since only 19% of eligible Medicare recipients used hospice before dying, it is possible that increased education about hospice availability will lead to better comfort care as well as decreased costs.

Daniel Callahan in his 1985 book, *Setting Limits: Medical Goals in an Aging Society,* encourages us to look at the concept of setting limits to how long and how much care will be given, and paid for by the government, to the burgeoning elderly population. Between 1980 and 2040, a 41% general population increase is expected, but there will be a 160% increase in those 65 or over. At the same time that lives have been extended, families have been having fewer children. The result is a negative shift in the ratio of old to young—less youthful caregivers for elders.

We are already being told that Medicare and other entitlement programs are only funded until 2030. While politicians are now trying to figure out the best ways to correct this problem, their focus has been how to get a better financial return on the collected monies for Medicare and Social Security, rather than in how these funds are being spent. Mr. Callahan is speaking of the possibility of government being forced to set some limits. Insurance companies are already setting limits of their own by reducing services. Is it possible that if we participate in making our own end-of-life choices, we will not only retain more control over our true destinies, but also begin to impact the "health care crisis" positively? If our elders have not explored these issues, it will be difficult to make such choices for them. But we can begin examining these ideas for ourselves and talk about them with our children.

This crisis of escalating costs and lack of personal control has already begun and is manifesting in the general discontent with our current health care system. The poor may obtain medical care with government assistance now; these costs are passed on to all taxpayers. The rich can afford enough insurance premiums to cover the portion of costs not covered by Medicare. But it is the large middle class that suffers the greatest difficulties. Those who are employed may have insurance premiums paid by their employers, as required by law in some cases, but the 20% not covered can add up to tens of thousands of dollars in serious illnesses, difficult to come by with middle-class income. In addition, many small businesses are closing because the cost of providing health insurance to their employees has decreased their profits. People who are self-employed must either spend the minimum of $150 - 200 per month for premiums with high deductibles or choose to have no health coverage. In the latter part of 2003, an updated survey showed that 43.6 million Americans have no health coverage—an increase of 6% in a short period of time.

Living without health care insurance leads to the seventh highest cause of death. Those who are uninsured fail to seek care despite symptoms indicating illness, and often die young because early detection was missed. Many elderly people are covered only by Medicare, with restrictions increasing monthly as to kinds of care and coverage. As the aging population increases, further demands will be made through taxes to maintain this level of government medical support.

Exploring these financial issues now illuminates our personal beliefs and ideas regarding how we value life. When is living longer more valuable than living well? How do we balance living a long life with living a good life? Examining these qualities may also bring balance to our health care system. As George Carlin said, "We've added years to life, not life to years."

EDUCATING OURSELVES AND OUR HEALTH CARE PROVIDERS ABOUT END-OF-LIFE ISSUES

As of 1998, only 7% of accredited nursing school programs required a course in ethics, and only five of 126 medical schools in America had a separate required course in dealing with the ethics of dying and death.

This is improving. In 2002, California passed initiative AB 487 that requires all doctors (except diagnostic radiologists and pathologists) to take twelve Continuing Medical Education units in pain management and care of the dying, prior to December 31, 2006. There are other courses and projects being offered, some required, that provide doctors and nurses with better understanding and skills in end-of-life care. The increased awareness on the part of professional caregivers, as well as that of health care consumers, will contribute to fewer bioethical dilemmas.

CHILDREN AT THE END OF LIFE

Possibly the most difficult area of end-of-life discussions concerns children who have terminal diagnoses. No parents want to see their child die. Abigail Trafford, in an article on children at the end of life in the *Washington Post*, writes, "Hospitals had no formal support system for families caring for a child who was going to die. There was no one health professional to offer consistent guidance throughout the...course...of illness. The medical team never mentioned a hospice program."

Most children who have chronic illness die in an intensive care unit and do not receive adequate pain medication. In addition, they may be hooked up to life-support equipment that extends their life while they are suffering. Part of the problem is that the rate of cure of certain kinds of leukemia, for example, has increased dramatically, providing hope to all who have this diagnosis. Yet, 30% of those stricken do die at a young age and they need palliative care and/or hospice care. The comfort care provided for adults is less likely to be provided for children because no one wants to give up hope.

Often the children sense they will die and try to talk about it, only to be hushed by parents and caregivers. Lifting the taboo of discussing dying and death may also help ease the suffering of children who are dying.

ENHANCED MEANING OF LIFE

Philosophers over the centuries have pondered the meaning of life. A few paragraphs here cannot possibly bring light to the subject in general. But allowing the bioethical issues discussed above to provoke thought and conversation with our loved ones can at least move each of us toward exploring our individual belief systems, formulating a plan for how we wish to die, and hopefully illuminating the reasons we want to continue living.

The future is no leap

We emerge there breath by breath

Even to greet death

C.R.

Seven

Quality of Life
and Medical Choices

*Only by a frank discussion of the very details of dying can we best deal with
those aspects that frighten us the most. It is by knowing the truth
and being prepared for it that we rid ourselves of the fear of the terra
incognita of death that leads to self-deception and disillusions.*

— Sherwin Nuland, *How We Die: Reflections on Life's Final Chapter*

LIVING WELL IS THE BEST REVENGE

When our ancestors were stricken with serious disease or the
cumulative results of having lived a long life, they were mainly
offered comfort care, since few remedies existed to sustain physical
life. Today, we have available a complex technology and medicine for
the diagnosis and treatment of disease and illness which allow life-
saving and life-maintaining procedures. However, the availability of
these interventions has created new medical considerations: *how to
weigh the effects of the medical choices against quality of life choices.*

If a hundred years ago the *fear of dying* haunted the hearts and minds of the extremely sick and those who loved them, we have added today the *fear of living* due to unexpected or unexamined outcomes from modern medicine. The emotional, psychological, and social impact of medical choices are upon us: how we will feel, act, think, and relate when faced with living and dying decisions.

Without extreme conditions, we seldom fully explore our heart's desires. What is most important in my life? What makes my life meaningful? For many, a medical crisis opens the door to the possibility of answering these questions and having discussions about the quality of life. So, can we use a potential or imaginary situation, rather than a crisis, to examine and improve our current quality of life?

QUALITY OF LIFE

The issue that creates the tension in making medical choices is usually the quality of life that the person currently has and would hope to maintain. We seldom think about quality of life until some of our physical, mental, emotional, or social roles and habits are threatened or curtailed. Few of us prepare for loss before it unexpectedly intrudes upon us. Yet, each of us lives on the brink of some kind of potential loss that would undermine the delicate balance—the quality—of our inner and outer lives.

Although quality of life will be different for everyone, its common elements may be separated into objective and subjective issues.

The objective points might include:

★   The level of ***pain and discomfort*** one is willing to endure
★   The ability to ***communicate*** with loved ones
★   The ability to ***function*** sufficiently to provide self-care or earn a living

★   The level of ***mobility and dependence*** on others
★   The ***length of time*** one is willing to live within any of these circumstances
★   One's age and general ***state of health***

The subjective factors could be:

★   A person's level of ***joy, enthusiasm and awareness***
★   The feeling of ***contribution*** to family and society
★   The belief that life itself has ***value***
★   The ability to discover or fulfill one's ***purpose*** in life
★   The level of ***acceptance*** of one's fate or destiny
★   The ***spiritual*** aspects, including belief in some kind of guidance for living now as well as an idea of what takes place after death

For example, Mr. Johansson may feel willing to be wheelchair-bound as long as he has full mental capacities and can communicate with others. Mrs. Waldsmith may want to continue living if she can take care of herself physically, even if she has chronic and intense pain. Miss Maple may feel strongly that she would not want to continue living if she didn't have full function of her body and mind. Mr. Esposito believes living with any physical limitation is of value as long as his family is able to care for him. And Mr. Brownstone states strongly that if there is any choice, he wants to continue living no matter what his abilities or future are.

Conversations about any of these issues now will help not only in considering future possible medical choices, but also to access what we really desire for our quality of life now. The medical choices in this chapter provide the opportunity to examine our feelings and to talk about our discoveries with family and friends. They may also create the opportunity to speak from the heart, express love, play more, and become adventurous. When death is sitting on our shoulder, the desire to live purposefully takes new precedence.

FRANK: "I AM FINISHED WORKING."

At 59, Frank planned to work at least until the normal retirement age of 65. He was a busy lawyer, putting in long days, and was always anxious to return to the office after his yearly two-week vacation.

Then he was diagnosed with colon cancer. It wasn't a tidy little tumor that could be surgically removed with little interference in his rigorous schedule. It was large, invasive, and required radiation and chemotherapy after the surgery. For the following months, Frank felt sick a large part of the time. His hair fell out. He had no energy. He had a lot of time to think and feel.

When the treatments were completed, he began the process of regaining strength and he retired. He realized that he had missed so many opportunities to spend time with his children and grandchildren. There were places in the world he had never seen. He began volunteering weekly at the cancer support group that had provided so much help for him during his months of treatment. He made himself available by phone to talk with any cancer patient who needed an experienced listener. Frank also returned to the religious life he had left behind years earlier. He and his wife began traveling. He offered to babysit his grandchildren. He expressed deep appreciation for each day. His cancer had become an awakening experience instead of one of fear.

EMERGENCY MEDICAL CHOICES

There is usually little or no time to consider the choices needed when a person has stopped breathing or when an organ has suddenly failed. It is during emergency situations that advance directives are the most valuable, if they are available, since leisurely conversations are not possible. Following are a few potential scenarios when choices might need to be made immediately.

* Shock, after an automobile accident, may indicate the need for immediate surgery to repair internal wounds. If the age and general health of such a person looks as though survival and recuperation is likely, such intervention would most often be chosen. But what if the person is elderly, dying, and emergency surgery might cause increased pain and discomfort? This would not be an easy decision.

* A woman finds her 85-year-old mother crumpled on the floor in her bedroom. She quickly checks to see if her mother is conscious and has a heartbeat. There is none. The choice is not clear, especially if there are no written instructions, if the daughter should seek resuscitation. The daughter could call 911 and risk injury to her mother from the intervention, or she could leave her mother lying on the floor and call the family physician and family members.

* A fifty-year-old man drops to the floor at his office because his heart has stopped beating. There is now the technical ability to try restarting his heart. There is no time for conversation. His co-workers may not know if he has advance directives but the choice is clear to call 911.

* A 75-year-old woman goes into cardiac arrest during surgery for advanced colon cancer. If her advance directives are present, the doctors know what to do. If not, questions must be asked before resuscitation takes place. The doctors must consider her potential to recuperate from the surgery, her other health problems, and her potential quality of life.

★ A child with advanced leukemia is recommended a third bone marrow transplant. The child says she is dying. The parents understandably don't want her to die. The decision is very difficult to make without support of others who have faced similar dilemmas.

One forceful conclusion comes from these scenarios: There are few, if any, clear-cut answers to "how best to handle the situation." Yet, even in the midst of uncertainty, the value of the advance directive is clear. (This seems to be especially true in high profile cases that receive media attention. One listens to the unfolding drama and thinks, "This is terrible! If only they had written their wishes, everything would have been all right." Most importantly, the conversations leading up to these decisions and documents will serve us well.

NON-EMERGENCY MEDICAL CHOICES

Medical choices may also be needed when specific kinds of life saving treatments or elective surgeries are suggested; yet these may also cause discomfort and pain. Following are a few examples of choices that might need to be made when there is time to have discussions.

★ Coronary bypass and valve-replacement are both lifesaving surgeries. As the arteries become progressively occluded or the valve gradually deteriorates, there is time to decide if or when such a surgery will take place. If the patient is in mid-life, such an intervention might be considered a miracle. If elderly and ill, it's success may cause a person to live for many years with pain and discomfort from non-heart-related ailments.

★ Modern screening procedures are able to detect cancer at early stages and the combination of surgery, chemotherapy, and radiation has provided additional years of healthy life for many people. The discomfort of the treatments is well worth choosing when the likelihood of recovery is projected.

★ Sometimes cancer is not diagnosed until it has spread to many parts of the body. Adding chemotherapy may only detract from what little time a person has left to take care of business and say good-bye. The choice is unclear without deep soul searching, the gathering of statistical information, and support from others.

★ An 80-year-old develops a heart condition that could be corrected by a pacemaker. She also has diabetes and is confined to a wheelchair due to a broken hip that could not be repaired. This intervention may cause her to live longer and in pain.

★ A 70-year-old woman has kidney failure resulting from a long-time illness. It is unlikely she will be a candidate for a kidney transplant due to her age. She is offered dialysis. When she finds out what is involved in receiving this treatment, she might decide not to go forward with it and to begin making preparations to die. She might also decide to have the treatment for a few months in order to get her affairs in order. A 70-year-old who has excellent health otherwise might choose to have dialysis for a longer period of time.

★ Some people may want to add or substitute alternative treatments to the recommended medical protocol, including herbs, homeopathy, fasting, and acupuncture. Beginning this research in the midst of the medical crisis may be difficult.

The outcomes from not taking the time to deal with these issues are extreme. On the one hand, the comforting sense that everyone involved did the best they could in preparing for the possibility of death; or on the other hand, if the person suffers, a sense of remorse and regret.

QUESTIONS TO ASK YOUR DOCTOR TO HELP EXPLORE MEDICAL CHOICES

If we become more comfortable discussing our feelings about the dying process, death, and the quality and value of life, we can assume and exercise our right to ask questions. We can gather information regarding the well being and future of our lives, treatments, and care. The following questions may be applied to any health condition and used even when the medical dilemma is not life threatening. Also, include your own additional or more specific questions to the following list related to a specific diagnosis, such as prostate surgery: How will it affect my sexual function? Eye surgery: What are the possible effects to my vision? Stomach surgery: How will it affect what I eat? And let us remember, no question is too trivial!

What do I need to know about the specific surgery or treatment?

Learning the details of the offered treatment is the first step. How long will it take? Where will it be administered? How may I expect to feel as a direct result of the intervention itself? How long is the recuperation from the surgery? What are the side effects from the treatment? Are there ways to alleviate these side effects? Will my insurance cover it? How much will it cost? Will I need it more than once?

What are the statistics of survival for someone my age and in my condition?

There are great differences between the recuperative abilities of a young and old person, of a body that is otherwise well and one that has many disease processes going on at the same time. Asking the doctor for this information is your right before you commit to a procedure or allow a loved one to go forward if you are speaking as an agent for health care.

Where can I learn statistical outcomes for specific interventions?

Ask your doctor first how you may learn more about the treatment being offered. If she doesn't lead you to this information, try the professional organizations that focus on the specific disease you are facing, such as the American Cancer Society or the Alzheimer's Foundation of America. Check the Internet for medical information, once you have located reputable sites, as well as for chat rooms where patients who have had the same diagnosis are willing to share their personal information.

The protocol for one kind of cancer treatment that has shown good results may be extended to other kinds of cancer. For example, a stem-cell transplant, which was initially used to treat ovarian cancer, has also been used for breast cancer without adequate research. This protocol requires intense chemotherapy and possibly radiation before the transplant even takes place, so it is very important to learn the outcome of others who have gone through such experience, as well as which diseases have responded best to such a treatment and which have not.

Will the surgery/treatment cure me, decrease my symptoms, or just give me more time?

If a patient is unable to eat but is expected to return to normal function, feeding may take place through a tube inserted either through the nose into the digestive tract or directly into the stomach. However, if a patient is sick and elderly and has lost appetite naturally, it is important to learn what the goal is of the tube feeding before agreeing to such a procedure.

Chemotherapy is most often administered with the aim of curing the patient of cancer. However, sometimes it is used to shrink the size of the tumor to increase comfort or function, or even to gain more time while the patient is still actually moving toward death. It will be very useful to know if a treatment is being offered to you for the purpose of cure or pain reduction.

How might I feel if I don't have the surgery/treatment?

Your decision to go forward with a specific treatment or surgery may also be influenced by learning the course of events that may be expected without the intervention. Undergoing open-chest surgery at an elderly age must be weighed against the symptoms of coronary artery disease. Questions must be asked regarding the possible outcomes of the surgery itself related to age and infirmity.

How long might I live without the surgery/treatment?

While we can never learn ahead of time when we will die, your doctor can make a reasonable guess as to the amount of time remaining if the diagnosis is clear. This information can be valuable in deciding if the surgery will provide enough extra time for you to get your affairs in order, or if you can accomplish what you want to do without the surgery.

Am I likely to survive the surgery/treatment in my present condition?

If a patient is failing in his or her ability to function or live without pain, a doctor may recommend a surgery to decrease the discomfort. Be sure to learn what the risks and benefits are of going forward with such an intervention if you or your family member is ill or infirm. The discomfort of the surgery may be greater than the ailment, and may also not be successful.

What other options are there, and what problems might I expect from each of those options?

Seek other opinions from other kinds of caregivers, if you have the time. There may be comfort measures available that your doctor doesn't know about. Hospice caregivers can be a valuable resource if you or your loved one is seriously ill.

If I were your (mother, father, daughter, son, spouse), what would you advise?

One would hope that a doctor would prescribe the same treatment for his patients, as he would give to his own family. Asking this question may invoke a more personal conversation, one that is not based on statistics or usual practice alone.

If I decide on an option you don't like, will you continue to be my doctor?

If we have an especially good relationship with a doctor, we might concede to his opinion without thought of our own feelings or need to seek another opinion or course of action. Yet it may not jeopardize our relationship if we speak frankly, expressing our concern and admiration for his care. How important is it to receive care from a familiar doctor as opposed to beginning with a new doctor who offers a more acceptable protocol?

QUESTIONS TO ASK YOURSELF ABOUT MAKING MEDICAL CHOICES

Do I want the time that the surgery may provide, even if it won't provide a cure?

What measurements of quality of life can you bring to this decision? Are you willing to live with any possible side effects of the surgery or treatment in order to live longer?

If choosing not to have the surgery/treatment means I may die soon, am I ready for that?

What will this mean for you, your family, and your future? Do you have your affairs in order? Are you afraid of death? Will you feel guilty if you decide not to have treatments? How will such a decision affect your family and friends?

Who can I talk with, if there is time, to help me make this decision?

Are any of your family members or friends willing to discuss your situation honestly? Are you interested in turning to professionals for this kind of help, such as a psychotherapist or member of the clergy? If you are in a hospital setting, are you willing to discuss your possible choices with the ethics team, social worker, or chaplain?

How do I feel when I consider these options and possible outcomes?

Are you clear about what your choices mean? Are your emotions making the decisions rather than the information you have gathered?

Are there alternative types of treatment I would like to explore before or alongside conventional medicine?

Researching resources for alternative treatments or therapies before a crisis occurs will open doors for future exploration, if the need arises.

ANNE-LISE

At 85, Anne-Lise still drove her car and was able to meet a few friends for lunch, nearby. Her husband had died ten years earlier and her two daughters were grown and married.

Without much warning, Anne-Lise began to have difficulties on her morning stroll in the neighborhood. She had shortness of breath and very little energy. She visited her doctor, who told her he wanted her hospitalized at once in order to do an angiogram. She resisted because of the suddenness, but the doctor insisted because he believed her care was urgent. He said that with just a few days in the hospital he would be able to correct the situation with angioplasty and that because the rest of her systems functioned well, she would be fine with the procedure. It turned out that her vascular system was so fragile that even the angiogram could not be performed, so he recommended she have heart bypass surgery.

Anne-Lise said no and that she wanted to go home. One daughter lived in another state and could not clearly understand over the phone what the ramifications of having the surgery or not having it might be. The daughter who lived in the same city also tried to learn what to expect from the surgery, and was told that without it her mother would no longer be able to enjoy her current lifestyle and that she would continue to weaken. It was likely she would die before too long.

One of Anne-Lise's long-time friends insisted that Anne-Lise go ahead with the surgery, as she knew others who had survived it without problems. The daughters said it was up to their mother to decide. No further opinions were obtained.

Anne-Lise had the surgery, followed by a slow recuperation. She said she didn't realize beforehand how she would feel afterwards. She became angry and cranky and later depressed. The daughters took turns staying with her, along with skilled nursing care. Medication for the depression helped somewhat, but she never regained the active life or the mental clarity she had previously enjoyed.

A year later she suffered a major stroke and continues to live with 24-hour nursing care. Her financial situation has allowed her to remain at home, though there has been a frequent turnover of the nurses, requiring the daughters to locate new caregivers and monitor her care. At times Anne-Lise has needed medication to calm severe agitation, heal bedsores, or halt the development of pneumonia. She cannot talk and does not recognize her family members.

Her daughters now wonder what the course of Anne-Lise's life might have been had she not had the life-sustaining heart surgery. Since they had not felt comfortable discussing the future ramifications of the surgery beforehand with their mother, or with the doctor, they have often felt anxious and responsible for the compromised quality of life their mother has lived for the past four years.

MEDICAL CHOICES FACED BY ANNE-LISE AND HER FAMILY

The above story shows the complexity of choices and the unknown outcomes that we may face with a loved one. First, did Anne-Lise want any treatment at all? Could she request or demand that she be allowed to die—as would have been the case before the introduction of bypass surgery? Whose shoulders would the responsibility of that choice lie upon? Whose input to Anne-Lise was the strongest—her doctor's, her daughter's or her friend's?

Anne-Lise made the decision to have the surgery, but after the stroke was not competent to make any future decisions about her care. When she suffered pneumonia on several occasions, she was always treated with antibiotics because these kinds of choices had not been discussed before her stroke. Her daughters did not feel comfortable to withhold treatment, even when they believed it was prolonging her discomfort.

Because Anne-Lise was very comfortable financially, she was able to stay home with round-the-clock care over a period of years. For others with only a moderate income or savings, there would also have been choices regarding care in an institutionalized setting. Without savings, the need to use Medicaid would further reduce the range of the kinds of care available.

MEREDITH

Meredith loved to dance and was delighted when she met a man who was willing to take lessons and go dancing weekly. They were both 75 and without major health issues until Meredith began to feel exhausted after dancing, exhaustion that increased with time and in severity as the weeks passed. She was diagnosed with vascular insufficiency and told she needed bypass surgery.

Since she had been a nurse until her retirement, Meredith was well aware of how much energy it would take to recuperate from the surgery itself at her age. In addition, she was aware that no one knew for certain that the results would allow her to continue enjoying the level of activity she had experienced before her symptoms began.

She thought long and hard, discussing it with her physician son as well as her own cardiologist. She decided to take the risk and go forward. The surgery was successful and she is dancing again with her friend.

MEDICAL CHOICES FOR MEREDITH

Meredith had the same symptoms and the same surgery as Anne-Lise. Meredith was lucky. She made a good choice and had a good outcome. She was younger, more active before the surgery, and as a nurse may have been more aware of the possible outcomes and side-effects. She took the risk and it worked. Anne-Lise also took the risk, and the results are not easy to measure. She is alive. She is cared for. But it is difficult to know if she is satisfied with her quality of life since she can't communicate. These kinds of choices are never simple, but they are extra hard if we are making them for someone else. Without having clear discussions ahead of time, how will the family know how you want to be cared for if you become bedridden and unable to communicate?

LIFE AND CHOICE

Unless we have chosen a medical career, most of us don't have a lot of information about how the body functions internally and how it will one day stop functioning. Sherwin B. Nuland, MD, describes clearly and compassionately the many ways we are likely to die in his National Book Award Winner, *How We Die: Reflections on Life's Final Chapter*. His writing is poetic, literary and even humorous. His belief that facing this mystery will teach us how to live more deeply is woven through the stories of his patients and the medical conditions that brought them to his care.

Sometimes I'm like a balloon

Full and round and trapped

I wish I could let it out.

J.K.

Eight

Practical End-of-Life Tasks

Funerals serve both a ritual and practical purpose.
Their ritual purpose is to celebrate and remember the life
of the deceased and to help the survivors accept the death.
The practical purpose is simple; something must be done with the body.

— Constance Jones, *R.I.P. The Complete Book of Death and Dying*

PLAN NOW, DIE LATER

The choices of burial or cremation, to have a funeral or memorial service, and whether or not to donate organs are not what we want to think about in the middle of a medical crisis. By discussing these and a few other end-of-life tasks, we achieve two significant goals. First, we prevent problems later on, especially if death is sudden. Second and more importantly, this discussion is often an opening for the deeper issues and concerns that are hidden within these tasks.

SUDDEN DEATH

Edward was only 55. His family told me that while his body was still warm, the hospital was demanding they make decisions. "Who was their mortician? Did the deceased wish to donate his organs since he was so young?" The family had no idea. Once they got him to a mortuary, there were more questions. "Did he want to be cremated or buried?" No one knew. Next, "Did he want a silk-lined casket and a burial plot with a view?" All this while everyone was still crying.

Since Edward had been healthy, with no signs or symptoms of his impending heart attack, neither he nor his wife Janice had talked about end-of-life plans. The grief of his death was enough to cope with; trying to decide upon cremation or burial was more than Janice could bear.

The lack of this information is not unusual, especially when someone dies who is neither elderly nor ill. If a parent has never said, "I want the most elegant coffin available, and I have already selected and paid for it," or, "Don't you dare bury me in anything grander than a plain pine box," how are we to know what he wants or what his choice means to him at a deeper level? Will we feel guilty at choosing something less than the best or feel inadequate to understand what is "best?" Will we feel anxious at spending too much money or confused from not having spent enough time to learn their true desires? Will our financial resources be threatened by spending our own money because a loved one hasn't set money aside for her final resting-place? How can the remaining loved ones be in accord and not face personal differences and unnecessary conflict?

Discussing the family's practical preferences is the first step, and writing down these wishes, in detail, is the next.

In addition to our parents making it easier for us, we have the opportunity to make these decisions easier for our children as well as the possibility of creating greater intimacy by initiating these thought-provoking topics.

The following sections discuss practical end-of-life options and a beginning for the explorations needed for making the decisions. They also serve to elicit conversations and feelings concerning these issues with all those involved.

THE COST OF END-OF-LIFE TASKS

We can imagine a time, say a hundred years ago, when families bathed and dressed their "dearly departed," a local carpenter built a coffin, neighbors helped dig the grave, and the local preacher led the service. The financial cost was minimal. Since the early part of the twentieth century, those tasks have been relegated to professional mortuaries and morticians. The price tag has increased accordingly.

Three major conglomerates now own most funeral homes in the United States. Even if an establishment looks humble and family-owned, it is likely that prices are controlled by a parent company and are high. The *average* price for a funeral today ranges from $5000-10,000.

These high costs are being challenged in a variety of ways. Becoming aware of the following possibilities allows you to plan ahead, as well as pursue less costly and new pathways—which are actually old—in caring for a loved one's body.

> ★   ***The Federal Trade Commission*** created the Funeral Rule, which prohibits funeral providers from making untrue claims about products or services. The Rule also requires funeral directors to provide itemized costs over the phone. This allows the consumer to shop and compare

prices and services. You may ask for a general price list that not only includes all prices but tells what is legally required or not. Contact the FTC to receive a pamphlet describing their facts about funerals. See p. 252.

★   **Preplanned funerals** are not pre-paid. For $20-30, a one-time-only, per person fee, depending on the part of the country in which you live, you may register with your local preplanned organization and describe the kinds of services you desire. At the time of death, all the choices have been made, which avoids giving this task to loved ones during the time of crisis. Payment is not due until the services are rendered. The Funeral Consumers Alliance coordinates the non-profit, volunteer, local organizations around the country that have made agreements with mortuaries to provide the lowest prices possible. To find the organization in your area, contact the FCA. See p. 252.

★   **Caskets** may now be purchased directly by the consumer at 50-70% less than from a funeral home. Local casket companies can be found in the yellow pages. Casket and urn artisans, with prices ranging form $150 to $2000, including inexpensive materials such as pine, plywood, and cardboard, can be located through the FCA. See p. 252. Morticians may not be pleased at missing the opportunity to sell a casket with a high markup in price, but they are usually willing to work with families who want to use their other services.

★   **Family-directed funerals** are returning. This movement encourages family and friends to prepare the body together, to use their own transportation to drive the body to the mortuary or crematorium, and to create their own funeral or memorial service. They may also build the casket or box needed for transport. For detailed information, instructions and legal concerns, visit Jerri Lyons' website, Final Passages. See p. 252. Also read Julie Wiskind and Richard Spiegel's book, *Coming to Rest: A*

              Guide to Caring for Our Own Dead.

★   **Embalming** is the practice of injecting a formaldehyde-based fluid into the arterial system of the dead body. The purpose is to both disinfect and preserve the body. Some states require embalming in cases related to specific diseases. However, *embalming is neither necessary nor required,* and adds to your funeral costs.

CREMATION OR BURIAL

Some of us hold religious beliefs that provide guidelines regarding disposition of the body. When those guidelines are absent, we must make the decision ourselves, while we are alive; if we are dead, others must decide for us. Things to consider are available funds, cost differences, and our feelings and preferences concerning cremation or burial. Also, we need to know where to find these services and whether to pay for them now or later.

If burial is the choice, a location in a specific cemetery can be visited and purchased ahead of time. Some families purchase several adjacent plots so they can be buried side by side. A coffin can be buried in the ground or placed above ground in a mausoleum.

If cremation is desired, one can choose either an organization that does only cremation or a regular mortuary that offers both cremation and burial. Checking ahead of time may expose a surprising range of prices. (Some mortuaries charge a great deal less for cremation than cremation-only businesses, even thought their burial funeral packages may be very high.) Once the cremation has taken place, the ashes may be kept in a container at home, in a vault at a cemetery, or buried in a regular plot. The ashes may be spread over the ocean, either by the crematorium or by the family, or saved for a ceremony at a later date. Some states have regulations about spreading ashes over land.

"I DON'T CARE
WHAT HAPPENS AFTER I DIE."

Ted was a retired army captain. In his eighties he was diagnosed with several life-threatening illnesses, and the family knew they must begin to make plans. Ted was not interested in these discussions, even though he acknowledged he was dying and would say, "You decide. I don't care what happens after I die." Periodically the subject was raised, followed by the same response.

As time passed, his wife and daughter decided to make arrangements and put a deposit on a gravesite with a great view of the ocean in a military cemetery. He supported their choice. Some weeks later, Ted asked his daughter to drive him out to the burial site. He got out of the car with help, looked around, nodded, and said he was ready to go. He remained quiet all the way home.

The next morning he gathered the family and announced with a new energy and sparkle in his eyes, "I don't want to be put in the dirt with a bunch of dead soldiers. I want to be cremated and have my ashes scattered at sea near our old beach home."

New arrangements were made. The family was relieved that he made the decision. He died peacefully within a few weeks, and the sea-side ceremony was exquisite. His grandsons paddled his ashes off shore on their kayaks. A young friend played taps on his trumpet. A seal frolicked along the shoreline as the family members waved their good-byes.

It is important to know that only immediate family members—spouse, children or parents—can request cremation for another if that wish is not written down in a will or advance directive.

RITUALS AT THE TIME OF DEATH

No matter what method of disposal is chosen, there is still the opportunity to sit for a time with the body of your loved one. This helps to increase acceptance of death and to allow others to say a final good-bye. Some people choose to bathe and dress their loved one. This is often part of a larger ceremony in which family and close friends can express their love, respect, and grief. Considering this possibility ahead of time creates the opportunity for such an experience to take place. Others may prefer viewing the body in a more formal mortuary setting in an open casket, or less formally in its freezer storage.

Because death has so commonly taken place in hospitals, the age-old custom of spending time with the dead body is not practiced as often. The healing benefits of this and other rituals are missed. It is also important to know that such a ritual can take place in the hospital when coordinated with the staff and mortician services.

TO GIVE OR NOT TO GIVE YOUR ORGANS OR TISSUES

If you die while you are relatively healthy, you can donate your organs and tissues to others. The lists of severely ill people who are waiting for healthy organs and tissues are long, now that technology has provided the opportunity for transplantation. How do you feel about the thought of having an organ removed from your body at the time of death? Does posing this question lead you to psychological and spiritual considerations, or to the possibility of public philanthropy? Within this decision we again encounter the complexity and mystery about issues concerning our body and our inner lives.

Dr. Paul Pearsal offers provocative ideas regarding the energy that organs carry into their new recipients in his book, *The Heart's Code: Tapping the Wisdom and Power of Our Heart Energy*. Based on his own experience of receiving a bone marrow transplant as well as hundreds of interviews with organ recipients, Dr. Pearsall suggests that some portion of the donor's energy travels to the new host. Reports of changed preferences for food, music and entertainment, as well as general attitude and personality shifts, led him to explore the kind of energy and memory carried by the heart. While his studies have led to new ways of enhancing immune system response and making healthy choices in life, his stories provide fodder for discussing your own thoughts about organ donation. (Dr. Pearsall advocates organ donation.)

Because the demand for transplants outweighs the supply by three to one, organs that are not perfect or young are now being used to provide increased time and health for those in need. A person who is 60 or 70 will be low on the list for receiving an organ since younger people are considered more likely candidates. Knowing this may encourage us to be willing to donate an organ even if we are not in the prime of life. (It should also make us ask very detailed questions if we are considering receiving an organ, making sure we know what age or quality of an organ we will get.)

The opportunity to have an organ actually donated is most likely to occur in case of accident, and that is why there is a place to mark this choice on your driver's license. You can also download a Uniform Donor Card, from the Red Cross. Many of your questions may be answered by exploring the websites listed under Organ and Tissue Donation. See p. 261. Your wishes may change as you age or become ill and should be updated on your license and in your advance directives. Most important, your wishes must be discussed with your family.

Some people also feel inclined to have their entire body

donated to science if they believe something can be learned from their particular physical history. This information needs to be communicated clearly and in writing to family members and close friends, including the specific institution to which the body should be delivered. The institution itself must be in agreement before the death occurs. Most mortuaries are compliant with such wishes and will see that the body gets delivered to the appropriate location.

AUTOPSY

There are medical and legal requirements related to autopsy, the surgical dissection of a body to determine cause of death. In normal circumstances, the family (or the deceased in his written advance directive) must give permission for an autopsy to be performed. However, if a person has not been seen by a doctor within six months and dies suddenly or without apparent cause, or if there is suspicion of homicide, an autopsy may be legally required. There are variations from state to state.

Some people and some religions have strong feelings about being buried intact. Discussions that include how we feel about the care of our body after death also lead to thought-provoking, spiritual considerations. The decision that is made about autopsy must also be included in the advance directives.

CALLING FAMILY AND FRIENDS

Who do we want to be *notified* of our death? Who do we want to be invited to the funeral or memorial? (These lists may not be the same.) A list of people complete with addresses and phone numbers, to notify or invite prevents important friends from accidentally being forgotten. Creating such lists now also serves as a reminder to see or contact people you have not been in touch with, with whom you've had dissension, or from whom you've become estranged.

JOHN: "HAVE THE MILLERS DIED?"
"DID WE GO TO THE EINAR'S FUNERAL?"

At 93, my Dad's memory is not good in present time. But he spends much of his waking hours reminiscing about his youth and his old friends. Listening to him each week wander through these memories, I have learned that when there has been no formal closure, such as a funeral or memorial, my Dad cannot hold the information that a friend has died.

I realized how many of my parents' friends whom they had known for half a century had simply "faded away." Distant relatives or caregivers often failed to notify my parents of the deaths of their friends.

CELEBRATIONS

There are several types of celebratory events that help the family and friends of the deceased to process the loss and celebrate the life. Discussing the ideas and wishes for the type of ceremony ahead of time can not only aid our loved ones in going forward during a difficult transition, but also allows us to participate in the planning of the rituals, food, music and location of the celebration. We may even choose to write our own obituary.

A funeral usually takes place within a few days of death, and often has the body present in the casket, which can be either open or closed. The original religious purpose of the funeral was to help the soul move on to the next life. It also provided closure to the life by helping the friends and family share the grief of loss.

A memorial service usually takes place within a month of the death. Several memorial services may be held if the deceased lived in different areas over a long period of time, or traveled widely. A memorial service focuses on recalling and witnessing the life of the person who has died. The ceremony offers the opportunity for people to share deep feelings and humorous anecdotes that honor a life well lived. There is usually the sharing of food and drink and a sense of festivity, since the initial shock of loss has passed.

Living memorial celebrations are sometimes held before death, by people who know they are dying but still feel well enough to gather with friends and family. This allows the commemorations to be heard by the dying person and also provides the opportunity to say good-bye.

EPITAPHS, EULOGIES AND OBITUARIES

An *epitaph* is an inscription on a tomb or grave in memory of the person buried there. It can also be a brief statement or poem commemorating the person and could be read or recited at a funeral or memorial service.

A *eulogy*, literally "good words," is a speech usually given at a service that recalls the accomplishments of the person who died, as well as expresses the feelings of the person offering the eulogy. These talks can inspire the guests as well as provide solace.

An *obituary* is the notice of a person's death, usually printed in the newspaper, containing biographical information, the cause of death, and names of surviving relatives. It is usually written by a close family member, but can also be written about oneself ahead of time. The mortuary can help you write and place an obituary in your local newspaper on a specific date.

WHEN FAMILY AND FRIENDS LIVE FAR AWAY

Because both my parents lived long lives, most of their friends, brothers, and sisters had already died. The friends who were alive were too old or ill to travel to a service. The next generation had moved to many different cities throughout the United States. My father's descendents were still in Denmark. I decided to bring the memorial service to them.

For each parent, I wrote a one-page eulogy and printed it on paper with a colorful border. Then I sifted through old family albums—healing for me—and selected photos that showed each of them at the various stages of their lives. I arranged a page of photographs and had them photocopied, in color, so that both the modern color photos could be enjoyed and the older sepia-toned prints could convey their time in history.

I mailed the packets containing the eulogies and photographs to all of the remaining family and friends. I also placed my father's pages in standup picture frames, alongside a beautiful orchid, in the lobby of the nursing home where he had lived for four years. The caregivers and other visitors were able to learn more about him and express their feelings of condolence.

MAKING A LIST

An excellent way to organize the practical information related to end-of-life issues is to use *In the Checklist of Life: A Working Book to Help You Live and Leave This Life!* by Lynn McPhelimy. The guidebook provides spaces for lists of numbers, things, dates, locations, plans, memories, and your own obituary.

TAKING CARE OF BUSINESS

Considering and doing the practical tasks described in this chapter not only helps your survivors, but also provides the opportunity to experience the feelings that may be evoked by picturing yourself gone: Who will you miss? What have you not accomplished? What places have you not visited? See the exercise called "Writing Your Own Eulogy" on p. 201.

Softly rain drizzles
It cleans my face
Nothing blocks the heavy rain
Tears roll to the ground

M.M.

Nine

Financial Issues

What you need to know and believe is that when you have taken care
of others, you have responded to the higher values of your existence—
people first, then money.

— Suze Orman, *The 9 Steps to Financial Freedom*

WHOM DO WE TRUST?

It would seem that creating one's end-of-life financial documents is a simple task to accomplish. We know that doing so will make it easier for our survivors to carry out our wishes. There are guidelines available for us in books, from attorneys and estate planners, and in a variety of courses.

And yet, close to *60% of all Americans die without wills or trusts.* Even if we have not gathered great wealth, a will or trust is helpful to our family members, especially during their time of mourning and upheaval. Describing the location of our valuables, documents, bank accounts and other resources can also help our loved ones proceed after we die.

Believe it or not, the following responses are commonly heard when asked the question, "Do you have a will or a trust?"

- ★ "I don't need to do that now, I'm too young."
- ★ "I don't really own enough property to warrant a will."
- ★ "I don't know the difference between a will and a trust or which kind I need. I'll look into that one of these days."
- ★ "I don't need a will or a trust. If I die, my wife will get everything. If we both die, our daughters will get everything."
- ★ "If I don't have a will, maybe I won't die."

In addition to what we will leave behind, there are many ways to provide more help to our family while we are alive. Estate planning helps our heirs save on inheritance taxes and shows how to design our estate to avoid probate fees. Many disagreements, bruised feelings and resentments could be avoided by taking these measures; yet here are even more reactions to estate planning:

- ★ "I don't want to give money to my children now, it may spoil them."
- ★ "I may need some of this money before I die. You never know what will happen."
- ★ "My children don't want to think about me dying so I don't want to bother them with all of this."
- ★ "I don't want to die. This makes me think about it."

CREATING FINANCIAL DOCUMENTS AS TOOLS FOR CONTEMPLATION

Preparing a will or trust allows your finances to bring light to your values. Sharing the following questions with your family and friends may help you learn from one another, as well as to decide what step is appropriate to take first.

★ Whom do you value?

★ What do you value?

★ Who deserves any or all of your assets after you die?

★ How may your money and other holdings benefit others in the best way?

★ How might you like to use it differently while you are alive?

★ Are there better ways to make your money grow?

★ Can you afford to give money to your loved ones now while they can use it to build homes and raise young families? Will it benefit them more now than later?

★ Are there family members or friends that you think should or should not be listed in your will because of estrangement? Do you have time or the inclination to initiate reconciliation?

★ Is there time to develop a new career?

★ In considering your current finances, might you make changes now to earn more?

★ Do you want to work less and spend more time with friends or hobbies?

★ Are there philanthropic interests you could begin developing now?

★ Can you use this opportunity to acknowledge how well you are doing?

Remember: No one has been known to say on his deathbed
that he wished he had spent more time at the office.

ESTATE PLANNING

The following brief discussions of financial documents are here to provide a language that will facilitate our financial conversations with family members and lawyers. Estate planning involves the creation, conservation, and eventual distribution of our real and personal property. Everyone needs a will. Some people need both a will and a trust. Areas of concern that will help us decide what kind of planning is needed include our health, marital situation, dependents, the status of beneficiaries, the risks involved in daily life, as well as age.

Wills

A will is the cornerstone of estate planning. It allows us to name an executor, the person(s) who will see that our wishes are carried out; to specify guardians for minor children, and to distribute financial assets and personal gifts to others.

A will is simple to create and can be done without outside help. There are books, computer programs, and classes to provide guidance in creating a will. A lawyer may also draw up a will.

Wills should be written or amended as often as needed and should be updated when life-changing events take place, such as marriage, divorce, moving, birth or adoption, or death of a beneficiary.

Probate

If the assets listed in the will must change title, such as when a house is left to a child or the contents of a bank account are left to a friend, the will must go through *probate*. Probate is a process in which a judge must authenticate the will and change the titles before dispersal of the assets takes place. This can take from six months to two years during which time nothing can be done with the property. It can also be expensive.

There are a number of ways to avoid probate if the estate is relatively small, such as creating *joint-titles* on deeds, bank accounts, and insurance policies. This allows both parties, for example a mother and daughter, to write checks on an account, both before and after either of them dies. Another way is to set up accounts with *pay-on-death* designations, which gives exclusive control to the account holder during life, but transfers it directly to the beneficiary upon presentation of a death certificate.

Making tax-deductible gifts from each parent of up to $10,000 per year to children and grandchildren can at least decrease the amounts of money that will be taxed and liable for probate. If the estate is large or complicated, a trust should be created.

Trusts

A trust states who controls our assets while we are alive, and what will happen to them when we die. It must be created with outside assistance and should be considered for the following reasons:

✧ To provide continuing care and education of minor children and grandchildren
✧ To provide income for a living spouse
✧ To provide care for a dependent or incompetent adult
✧ To provide professional management of assets
✧ To minimize estate taxes if the combined estate of husband and wife exceeds one million dollars (through 2003, and $1,500,000 through 2005).
✧ To avoid probate

A trust allows our assets to be easily passed on to our heirs, as well as to create a legal way of providing for the above-mentioned situations. It can seem expensive, but the cost must be measured against the benefits provided for those we love.

What happens when we die and have neither a will nor a trust?

✧   State laws will go into effect and distribute the property.

✧   If children are young, the state can also determine guardianship.

Every family has different needs

The first step is to determine the type of will to create and if a trust is also necessary.

✧   Read the material suggested under FINANCIAL ISSUES on p. 250.

✧   Answer the questions on p. 99.

✧   Listen closely to the financial stories of friends and relatives as they experience the death of loved ones.

✧   Make notes of what points were missed and what traumas occurred.

✧   Note when and how resolution of financial issues happened without problems.

✧   Take a class on estate planning from a local college.

✧   If more clarity is needed, consider consulting a professional estate planner to draw up your documents.

If you decide to meet with an estate planner gather all existing documents, including bank accounts, investments, deeds, retirement plans, and insurance policies. In addition, consider plans for future health care and retirement needs and make a list of questions before making an appointment.

The final and most important step is to do it! It will not matter if the decisions have been made and the bank accounts gathered if the will or trust has not been created, signed, and its location communicated to family members.

FINANCIAL POWER OF ATTORNEY

Before a parent becomes incapacitated and cannot sign checks or conduct business, he or she, the principal, may want to name an agent by creating a Financial Power of Attorney. This will allow the agent to transact most business for the principal. States vary as to what is excluded.

* ★ This document must be created when the principal is mentally competent and should only be done when the agent is considered to be extremely trustworthy.
* ★ It can be beneficial alongside a living trust to cover areas such as retirement funds or personal care that are not included in the trust. Most often it is used when an elder or ill person is not physically able to write checks or sign documents pertaining to health or business issues.
* ★ There are many options that can be employed in this document, such as: length of time (e.g. for use only during a medical recovery), adding alternate agents; specifying which kinds of business can or cannot be conducted; or creating co-agents who must act jointly.
* ★ This power ceases with the death of the principal. This is important to remember in case you are planning to write checks on a parent's account for burial needs. Having joint title on at least one checking account would also be beneficial. You may have both arrangements.

LONG-TERM CARE INSURANCE (LTC)

The average cost for care in a nursing home is approximately $50,000 per year, nationally, and more in urban areas such as Los Angeles and New York. Few of us have assets to cover this kind of care for very long. Neither Medicare nor health insurance covers long-term care.

Medicaid will pay for long-term care if the family is destitute.

In the past, many families "spent down" their savings to qualify for Medicaid. That possibility may change as a bill has been introduced that makes giving away assets in order to receive Medicaid a criminal offense. In addition, using Medicaid creates limits as to the kinds of facilities available for your parent—often the more appealing sites do not accept Medicaid.

The problem is that long-term care insurance is expensive and its premiums increase with the passage of time. Financial advisors recommend that it be purchased during one's mid-fifties, decades before it is likely to be used. For example, a person in good health at age 54 can get a policy for $954 per year. The same policy purchased at 65 would cost $2,580. However, AARP researched LTC policies and found some of them increased the premiums over time, even though the major point for early purchase is to retain the same fee. Most people don't think about its purchase until they or a parent become ill; at that time the policy is not even available. Only 6% of Americans have long-term care insurance.

LTC insurance is not the ideal solution to our living many years with chronic health problems, but it must be considered in end-of-life care planning. There are current plans to provide LTC to government workers and members of the armed forces and plans to initiate tax credits for the cost of this insurance. LTC insurance is an area in need of advocacy to change its cost, establish how and when it may be obtained, and to stimulate thought regarding new ways to provide care for aging or chronically ill people.

MONEY TALKS

As we prepare our financial documents, we can let them speak to us of our values, plans, dreams, and relationships. It will help to keep notes of the thoughts and emotions that float by while considering how we use and will disburse our assets.

Along the way, I slipped and fell.

There were no rocks or stones.

It was sand that dropped me in my tracks, I know.

Now what?

Time is not on my side

But I want to stand again.

And there is a stick of wood; it's mine.

H.N.

Ten

Advance Directives

Advance directives have been signed by less than 15%
of the American public, despite widespread publicity and discussion.
—— Daniel Callahan, *The Troubled Dream of Life: In Search of a Peaceful Death*

PLANNING AHEAD

Now that you've explored some of the fears that keep you from talking (chapters Four and Five), and gathered some information about the bioethical, medical, practical and financial end-of-life issues (chapters Six through Nine), you can begin to fill out your advance directives. First clarify your personal philosophy, which includes how you value life itself, the quality of life you want to maintain, and your hopes and dreams. This is the background for the specific plans you will be making. Then, you can discuss the formal documents that are commonly used and learn how to prepare them. It is important to remember that writing down your wishes in an advance directive is only the first step. Having conversations with your family, friends, neighbors, and doctors, so that they understand your philosophy, will be more likely to bring good help in a crisis than the written document alone.

Advance directives include the Durable Power of Attorney for Health Care, Living Will, Five Wishes, and in some instances the DNR (Do Not Resuscitate). These documents were created in response to modern medical technology's ability to revive people and keep them alive. Before this technology, severe illness or accident was likely to lead to death. Now there is often a choice. Most often, you will be able to participate in making choices about impending surgery or treatment. However, if you are unconscious or unable to communicate, these forms will help the person you designate to make the necessary choices on your behalf.

While the general public has become aware of advance directives during the last 25 years, the majority of the population have still not prepared their own documents. Even if they have, the documents too often may not be honored. This failure to fulfill people's wishes can be a result of vagueness in the writing of requests, documents that cannot be located, disagreements between family members, and fear of prosecution by hospital staff and doctors. Traveling state to state can bring different responses and different laws. Even if you have created a directive in California, and happen to have it with you, it may not be recognized in Arizona. There is also no consistent agreement between community residents and emergency caregivers (paramedics and emergency room physicians) about how to use these documents and where to find them.

Nevertheless, it is important to create these documents. Answering the questions on the forms can stimulate inner conversations about what you value in life and in death. In considering your death, you crystallize your philosophical and spiritual beliefs, enhancing your remaining days and years. Once you complete and distribute the directives, loved ones will have greater leverage to ensure that you get the kind of treatment you want or do not want, without guessing, in an already stressful time.

When advance directives have not been created, a spouse, parent or child can speak for their family member, if there is time to have conversation and make a decision, *and* if there is agreement between them. Also, it is even more important for couples who are not married, or cannot legally marry (same-sex life partners) to fill out the legal documents, as a distant blood relative could have legal power over a live-in mate.

DURABLE POWER OF ATTORNEY FOR HEALTH CARE

This document allows you to specify your medical end-of-life wishes. (It should not be confused with a Financial Durable Power of Attorney, described on page 103, which is related to legal and financial matters, not health issues.)

The Durable Power of Attorney for Health Care allows one to:

★ Select a *proxy (agent),* the person who will make sure health care wishes are carried out if one is unable to communicate. Choosing an agent represents the main difference between this document and a Living Will. A second proxy or agent (co-agent) may also be listed. It is very important that a proxy is trustworthy.

★ Request life to be maintained as long as possible, without regard to condition, chance of recovery, or the cost of treatment.

★ Request life-saving and/or life-sustaining treatment to be provided, unless the patient is in a coma or in a "persistent vegetative state." Two doctors, including the attending physician, will determine this state in their best judgment.

★ State that life is not to be unnaturally prolonged unless there is significant likelihood that both your physical and mental health can be restored.

★ State that resuscitation is not desired if the heart stops beating, unless there is a strong reason to believe good health can continue.

★ List in detail what kinds of treatments you may or may not want related to specific conditions, including general health, age, and family responsibility. These treatments may include, among others, gastric tube feeding if unable to eat, antibiotics, continued hydration, and surgery.

★ Give the proxy the right to authorize an autopsy, donate organs, and determine how remains will be disposed, unless otherwise specified.

The powers of the Durable Power of Attorney for Health Care have different time limits in different states. It is also very important to review it periodically to see if your wishes have changed with time.

You may also create a *naked* Durable Power of Attorney for Health Care, which gives the proxy complete power to make decisions if communication is impossible, rather than asking him to follow specific requests. This would be an option only if the proxy completely understands the patient's philosophical beliefs regarding life and death.

How are the forms created?

To create these documents, locate a form that is state specific. Be aware that if you have an accident or incur illness in another state, your wishes may not be honored. Forms can be obtained from:

◇ The Internet and books (see p. 222.)
◇ Hospitals, nursing homes, and doctors' offices
◇ The lawyer doing your financial estate planning

Discussion with close family members should precede filling in the forms. The forms may also be completed with a group of friends and family members and used as a point of discussion and communication. See exercise on p.181.

What do you do with the forms once they have been prepared?

✧   Give copies of the advance directives to the proxies (agents), family members, nursing home, doctors, lawyers, and neighbors. It is more likely that a neighbor will be the first on the scene than any of the others mentioned (if one become ill at home).

✧   Review it annually, or when significant changes occur, to see if your wishes have changed, and whether your selected proxies still seem appropriate.

✧   Replace all changed documents that have been given to others.

✧   Carry a wallet-sized card that indicates the location of the documents.

✧   Store electronically, at no charge, with US Living Will Registry. The documents will then be available directly by telephone to health care providers across the country, through an automated computer-fax system. See p. 222.

✧   Medic Alert produces jewelry with a phone number that transmits vital medical facts, including DNR, to the paramedics. Or, the requested information can be engraved on the jewelry. See p. 222.

Is creating the DPA for H enough to have your wishes carried out? No, it is not!

✧   All patients need advocates. See chapter 17.

✧   Doctors, and especially paramedics, are trained to save lives. If the situation is an emergency and communication is not possible, there is often not enough time to locate a document or a listed agent.

✧ Talking freely about feelings regarding this document to all of the people involved is important so that they understand your philosophy or spiritual point of view and are able to act as an advocate, in addition to following your specific requests.

✧ If you or a loved one is in a nursing home and gets transferred to a hospital, it is important that the advance directives travel with the patient. This should be discussed with nursing staff ahead of time.

When should you create this document?

✧ At 18 years of age. An accident can occur at any time. Before age 18, parents or guardians are responsible for making decisions for your health care decisions.

✧ If under 18, wishes can also be recorded so that parents will have the written support of a child who can't speak for herself.

FIVE WISHES

The non-profit organization, Aging with Dignity, created the Five Wishes document to be "user friendly." It reads less like a legal document and more like an organized but informal list of requests. It is very worthwhile to look at the Five Wishes document for ideas in formulating your wishes. As of mid-2003, it is considered to be legally valid in the District of Columbia and forty states. The Five Wishes document considers the following areas:

1. Choosing an agent (proxy) and alternate agents

2. Requesting the kinds of medical treatments desired or to be excluded and under what conditions

3. The kinds of comfort care desired

4.   How to be treated while unconscious

5.   Information for loved ones regarding a eulogy, funeral celebration, type of body disposal, autopsy, and organ donation

The document must be signed in front of two witnesses and in a few states, notarized. Visit the website of Aging with Dignity to download or order a copy of Five Wishes as well as to learn if your state considers the document as legally valid. See p. 22.

LIVING WILL

The Living Will is an informal document in which you can state desires about end-of-life medical care. It does not provide the opportunity to name an agent (proxy). A Durable Power of Attorney for Health Care or Five Wishes is therefore more beneficial, as long as detailed and specific wishes are included.

The term "living will" is generically used by some for advance directives because it was the earliest name for such types of documents.

DNR

The initials stand for *Do Not Resuscitate*. This document deals only with resuscitation, when the heart stops beating (cardiac arrest) or the person has stopped breathing (respiratory failure). Most nursing homes ask their patients if they want to sign one when they are admitted. Hospice caregivers usually require their patients to sign a DNR to make sure it is understood that the care being given at this point is palliative and not curative.

There is also a document less commonly used called a DNI (*Do Not Intubate*). This would indicate that a person might feel it is all right to be resuscitated but not to have life maintained by "tubes," such as a ventilator.

MARTIN: A LOVING TEAM;
NO LEADER; NO DOCUMENTS

Martin was a respected teacher and had a large circle of friends. When emergency surgery led Martin, at age 84, into a painful dying process, his "team" moved into place. They brought soft food and tried to feed him, though he wasn't hungry. They took turns sitting with him. The attending doctor recommended a feeding tube. He believed that with nourishment, Martin would recuperate from the surgery.

Martin had told his close friend Jane, who happened also to be a physician, that he wanted her to make his health care decisions if he became unable to communicate. However, he had never written down what he wanted, or legally appointed Jane as his agent. Jane could see he was close to death—that the feeding tube would only prolong the discomfort and pain he was now enduring. Martin's friends wanted him to continue living and argued with Jane, making her feel guilty for what she medically knew would be best. Jane didn't want to lose him either, yet she believed comfort care was the only practical and benevolent way of maintaining his quality of life, regardless of whether he lived or died.

Martin died, not very peacefully, within a few weeks, and the next difficulty began. He had verbally expressed the desire to be cremated but there were no available written documents. His friends knew he did not want to be buried. Without either immediate family—spouse, parents or children—or written instructions, the team learned he could not be cremated and that the state was required by law to assume responsibility of his body. When the memorial service was held two weeks later, Martin's body was still in a refrigerator at the county morgue. A distant cousin-in-law finally found a 25-year old, handwritten will of Martin's that requested cremation. A week after this document was presented, Martin's body was cremated.

Martin's team players were filled with love and concern and were available to give any needed help. If there had been group discussions ahead of time, especially including Martin before he became ill, his care would have taken a gentler path. Instead of trying to nourish him back to life, the focus could have been placed on better pain management and quality of life. If there had been a written document giving Jane legal responsibility to make medical decisions, as well as designating her as a team leader, there might have been less discord among the team members. Jane would also have been able to initiate the cremation process, decreasing the days and weeks of confusion after his death.

OUR DESTINY

Personal control over our destinies is what the supporters of advance directives hoped to solve as medical technology invaded that territory. Yet, there is a mystery that often introduces responses and idiosyncrasies that we can't even imagine when we are carefully filling out our forms.

Joseph was a responsible military man and had filled out his directives years before he became ill. He stated he wanted no life extension whatsoever. When almost every organ in his body was failing, he scratched out on a piece of paper, "Do anything to save me, please."

Meanwhile Dave, who had also requested no heroic attempts to save his life, was golfing in another state when he collapsed. He even had his directives with him but they were not valid there, so the paramedics revived him. Dave is still playing golf and thrilled that his requests were not honored.

Jean, on the other hand, had been in a nursing home for four years, had suffered several strokes, and could no longer speak or walk. When her heart stopped beating, a visiting doctor on call didn't even look for her available directives. He resuscitated her and then connected her to a ventilator. Jean's family was outraged. The doctor's response was that Jean looked well nourished and could still enjoy living.

As Daniel Callahan says in the *Troubled Dream of Life: Searching for a Peaceful Death,* "The art of managing human mortality will require moving back and forth between possibility and constraint, openness and limits, control and acceptance." As technology seemingly increases control by curing some diseases, it doesn't address the mysterious aspects of when life should end or whether it should continue. Advance directives won't solve the problem either, but they are still useful tools to explore our own feelings about life and death, as well as providing a language to work with in our medical, family, and social communities.

We are made of light

In a body to be lived

Then released again.

M.L.

Eleven

Caregiving

Because caregivers have touched...suffering and generosity...
they are given a vision of the whole, the world beyond self.
Helping others can become a calling from the far side of grief, a mandate to
assuage psycho-spiritual ghosts that remain long after the physical
tasks have been accomplished—or even in the midst of them.
Those who are touched by compassion discover life at its purest,
honoring the mystery of service and the value of each person.

—— Beth Witrogen McLeod,
Caregiving: The Spiritual Journey of Love, Loss and Renewal

WHO CARES?

Caregiving at the end of life is one of the most important issues
before us in the twenty-first century. The population over sixty-five
is expected to almost double by 2040, according to Daniel Callahan
in *Setting Limits*. In practical terms, this means:

★ The number of elders is increasing as the percentage of
   younger family members is decreasing.

★ *Everyone* is likely to provide care to a loved one, and possibly for a long time.

★ *Everyone* is likely to need care, and possibly for a long time.

★ More than 70% of Alzheimer's sufferers live at home, because most insurance does not cover custodial care. This can continue for many years.

★ Retiring at age sixty-five and living to be ninety-five leads to thirty years of slowing down physically and developing chronic diseases that don't kill but require care.

★ One in three women over sixty-five will develop cancer, requiring care during long courses of treatment.

The following further complicates the caregiving dilemma:

★ Many family members have moved to faraway cities leaving their parents or siblings without a core support system nearby.

★ Many families require both partners to work full-time and cannot personally give needed care without jeopardizing their own financial needs.

★ Geographical separation can also mask the need for care, as when distant loved ones say on the phone, "Everything is just fine," even when it is not.

★ Medical insurance companies, including Medicare, pay for surgeries, treatments and hospitalizations, but seldom cover care at home, or in nursing homes.

★ The cost of round-the-clock caregiving is affordable to very few.

★ Long-term care insurance, which does pay for care in nursing homes, is very costly, especially if it is not purchased early.

★ If we wait until the crisis occurs, parents are often elderly and may cling to their familiar homes and belongings.

★ If mental deterioration has begun, it is often impossible

to engage in conversations that would enable caregiving decisions to be made.

★ The resistance to talking about illness, dying, and death prevents families from exploring options ahead of time.

★ Emotional separations within families can prevent even the desire to care for a loved one in need.

★ Guilt over placing a loved one in a nursing home can lead to emotional suffering.

★ Not placing a relative in a nursing home can create upheaval for the rest of the caregiver's family.

PEARL: "EVERYTHING IS FINE JUST THE WAY IT IS."

Pearl is 85 years old, overweight, has chronic low-back problems, and forgets to take her medicine for high blood pressure and diabetes. She has lived in the same home for over 40 years, and now it is filled with clutter, dirt, dust, and a lifetime of memories. She calls her son John and daughter-in-law Brenda frequently asking for their help in the yard, and complains someone is stealing her kitchen utensils. She goes into detail about who the robbers are and how they have gained entrance to her home. On other days, she expresses surprise that the robbers have returned the missing items.

John, Brenda, and their two grown daughters, who have always been close to their grandmother, are deeply concerned and confused about how to provide care for Pearl. She refuses to talk about moving somewhere close to them where they can help her with errands and housekeeping. Because of her long-time heartiness, there had never been family discussions about what the future might bring before her

> *fears and dementia increased and her quality of health decreased. They are still without a solution.*

Discussing the implications of our inevitable need for receiving and giving care now can lead to new attitudes, the knowledge of available resources, and the possibility of developing community involvement to benefit all of us.

A NEW ATTITUDE ABOUT CARING

Many of us have heard a parent say, "I will do anything to avoid being in a nursing home," or "I don't want to be a burden to my children." Three questions underlie these pressing concerns:

★   What can we do to help our parents deal with their fear of incapacitation?

★   How will we help our children care for us when we are in need?

★   What are the alternatives to the extremes of nursing home care and the feeling of being a burden?

These lead to a fourth:

★   How can we see caregiving in a new light?

Henri Nouwen writes in *Our Greatest Gift: A Meditation on Dying and Caring,* "Caring is the privilege of every person and is at the heart of being human." Yet, in modern times, we have relegated caring to professionals who have been trained to care. While so many of us fear the lessening of our physical and mental capacities as we age or become ill, Nouwen suggests that we see these decreasing abilities as "gateways to God's grace." If we can create communities of caring, both the caregivers and those cared for begin to feel the same. Our greatest fears diminish. Fears of being found a burden or nuisance are allayed when heartfelt and loving people care for us. And when we can give care to others from our hearts, we diminish those same fears in ourselves. Nouwen also encourages us to seek help and community in giving care and not to make it an endurance test. "When we care together, the boundaries between receiving and giving vanish, and true community can start to exist."

CARING FOR LOVED ONES CANNOT BE DONE ALONE

The nuclear family can cope with flu season and broken arms. But what happens when cancer is diagnosed, resulting in a year of treatments; dementia takes over the mind of a once bright parent; or one of many diseases relegates an active family member to a wheelchair? The larger community must be included in order to:

- ★ Find the right place for our loved ones to live if we cannot care for them at home
- ★ Find specific kinds of caregivers to assist us at home
- ★ Obtain financial assistance
- ★ Rejuvenate ourselves so we can continue giving care
- ★ Discover and locate special equipment or medicines that we may not even know exist
- ★ Deal with the guilt and fear that can surround a long-term caregiving situation

There are hundreds of thousands of people in our country giving and receiving excellent care. But it cannot be done in isolation. When a loved one is in a medical crisis, family members can't clearly make all the decisions needed. Sometimes disagreements between family members can increase the problems. When illness continues over long periods of time, fatigue sets in, no matter how deep the love. Without help, both the patient and the caregiver are subjected to extreme stress, guilt, anger, and depression. At the same time, turning complete care over to strangers deprives family members the experience of deep intimacy and growth that caregiving brings. Help for the helpers is available, and the potential for new kinds of assistance is on the horizon.

SOURCES OF CAREGIVING HELP

Following are categories of places and people to turn to when we need more help than our own household can supply. For the actual names and contact information of many of these resources, see p. 232.

Agencies: Some are run by the government, some by churches, some by people who have gone through difficult and rewarding caregiving situations. There are agencies that will help in understanding specific illnesses, obtain financial assistance, provide equipment, and select residential or day-care centers.

Care managers or case workers: One of the most valuable resources available to families giving or receiving care. Often social workers or nurses, they can be located through hospital discharge departments, local community centers, a care-manager organization, or senior resource guide. A care manager can help find places to live, part-time care, equipment and other services.

Clergy: Religious organizations can offer many sources of caregiving. In addition to spiritual guidance and prayers, churches may also provide volunteer help and support groups.

Friends and the larger family: When illness and hardship strike, it is often difficult for those outside the immediate family to know what to do. Asking friends and other family members to help give care, run errands, or rub shoulders can provide help as well as offering the opportunity to participate.

Home health care: Nursing care can be provided at home a certain number of days per week as needed. Medicare covers some of these services.

Hospice: Even if a loved one isn't near death and ready for hospice care, a local hospice can provide guidance to other areas of support, as well as help determine when their care will be needed.

Other caregivers: Talk to those who have cared for their loved ones to learn what helped them and what made it difficult.

Resource guides: Many communities have gathered all of the known services into a publication that is distributed through senior centers, churches and doctor's offices.

Support groups: There is a support group for almost every illness, as well as for those who have aging parents, sick children, suffered the loss of a child, or loss of a spouse. Knowing that others specifically understand your situation can help keep one's emotional life intact—especially if care must continue over a long period of time.

REMODELING CAREGIVING

It is time to put on our thinking caps and create new ways to provide care for one another in our near futures. Nursing homes, board and care facilities, 24-hour home care, retirement communities, three-tiered or not, are surely not the only solutions. What most of these existing models provide is isolation from what was once known, whether it is removal from one's home, neighborhood, or circle of friends.

Cost for a residential setting with some type of care provided is at least $3500 per month for one person. How could that amount of money be used in a different way to provide good care, a homey environment, and people with whom we are happy to live near or with? Following is a list of ideas.

    ★   *Communal sharing of caregiving:* As we let go of our larger homes, can we consider moving to apartment houses or neighborhoods near friends or family where one nurse, one housekeeper, one driver could also live and help meet needs?

    ★   *Providing homes and income to caregivers:* Can we match the needs of those capable of giving care to those who need it, given that many people are living alone and without purpose, while still physically capable of providing care to others?

★ ***Matching caregivers with those needing care:*** Are there new ways to connect the givers and receivers together in local communities, without agencies, and still be safe?

★ ***Planned board and cares for friends:*** Instead of living with strangers, can we think ahead about the people with whom we might like to share a home and resources?

★ ***New business opportunities:*** Are there hidden opportunities and solutions to caregiving dilemmas that can lead to new businesses of providing care? Could these be funded partially by grants or donations?

L'ARCHE

In 1964, Jean Vanier founded the first L'Arche (the Ark) community, north of Paris, for mentally and physically disabled adults. There are now over 100 L'Arche communities, including 13 in the United States. The caregivers, known as assistants, do not need health care credentials. They live with the patients, known as core members, five days a week and receive room and board, plus a salary of about $500 per month. The philosophy is that the assistants and the core members live in equality, both giving and receiving, both healing and being healed. Most of the budget to run such a community comes from grants, government funding, and private donations.

Can such principles be applied to other groups in need? How about elders being paired with younger people, even those only a decade younger but still capable of working and driving? What if people who were in transition, say after a divorce or death of a spouse, could live in such a community for a month or a year?

Learning more about L'Arche may provide ideas for new systems of caring for our elderly and our ill. See p. 238.

COHOUSING: A POSSIBILITY FOR CAREGIVING

Cohousing is a type of collaborative housing that attempts to overcome the alienation of modern subdivisions in which no one knows his neighbors and there is no sense of community. Residents have their own living spaces and share communal dining and recreation facilities.

Some groups have planned the actual buildings and requirements ahead of time and built them. Others have chosen existing structures such as an apartment building or a group of houses.

Could the principles of these communities contribute to new ways of caregiving? The concept was first developed in Denmark and was brought to the United States by Kathryn McCamant and Charles Durrett. Learn more about their work on p. 238.

SHARE THE CARE

Cappy Capossela and Sheila Warnock describe their experiences in gathering friends to provide care in their book, *Share the Care: How to Organize a Group to Care for Someone Who is Seriously Ill*. Their story began when a therapist friend invited them to discuss the care needs of Susan, a friend they all had in common, who was undergoing cancer treatments. This first meeting led to over three years of involvement between twelve women and Susan, in which each took turns driving her to chemotherapy, helping with her children, keeping the household functioning, providing food, paying bills, and ultimately preparing for the wedding of Susan's daughter.

When another friend was diagnosed with cancer, Cappy and Sheila gathered a second "Funny Family" to provide the needed care. Their resulting book is filled with charts and instructions for accomplishing such a goal, as well as showing how the caregivers received just as much benefit as the friend who was receiving the care.

Share the Care also provides a foundation for ways we might care for one another without the aspect of a serious illness to draw the support.

AND THOU SHALT HONOR

On March 9, 2002, PBS aired a two-hour documentary on family caregiving called *And Thou Shalt Honor.* The film tells the stories of the caregivers, those they care for, and the professionals who struggle with an under-funded and often misunderstood system. The video or DVD can be ordered and used for education purposes. See p. 234.

THE EDEN ALTERNATIVE

Bill Thomas, MD, is a geriatrics doctor who is determined to revolutionize nursing-home care. The components of this new way to care for elders includes treating the caregiving staff in a more humane way; giving the elders a voice in their care and routines; and making the place where they live rich in plants, animals and children. Dr. Thomas also believes that growth continues and must be encouraged at any age.

Scenes of the Eden Alternative may be seen in *And Thou Shalt Honor* as well as on a PBS News Hour interview with Jim Lehrer. More information about how to "Eden-ize" existing facilities, or to create new ones may be found at the Eden Alternative website. See p. 233.

WE CARE

Serious illness can be diagnosed at any age and requires so much more care than just the treatments that are prescribed. Despite anti-aging medications, exercise, and vitamins, most of us will require care temporarily and some for months and even years. In addition, some will require care and assistance related to natural disasters, political attacks, and automobile accidents, regardless of age or health. If we begin to think about what these situations will require now, we will have a better sense of the options that are available before a crisis occurs.

He cannot bring up her fear

She is afraid of being alone

He cannot see that she is not angry at him

They chase one another in ordinary circles

They love each other

L.H.

Twelve

Good Grief

For everything there is a season,...
a time to weep, and a time to laugh;...
a time to mourn, and a time to dance;....

—— Ecclesiastes 3:4

BEREAVEMENT, GRIEF, MOURNING, AND RELIEF

What is it that happens when we suffer a loss? We feel something, and often we don't know what the feeling is, what is causing it, how to make it go away, or even if we want it to go away. Oftentimes it shows up unexpectedly and then retreats. Sometimes it is so overwhelming that denial steps in to quell its pain.

Any loss can induce feelings of grief—we get fired, leave our hometown, graduate from college, break up with a boyfriend, or have a hysterectomy. We mourn what has been left behind. We feel anxiety about what is to come. We feel confused about the choices we have to make. We feel angry about the upheaval.

When the loss is due to death, the grief can feel unbearable–even more so when daily life is completely interrupted, as when a child or a spouse dies, or when we learn that our own death is imminent. And yet there are times when the loss is a relief, welcomed, and even reason for celebration.

There are at least four aspects to the reactions that accompany a loss:

Bereavement is the emotional or psychological state we are in when we suffer a great loss, especially death of a loved one. An employer may offer a bereavement leave, not unlike a maternity leave, because it is known there is a new and different phase of life at hand, and the person needs time to adjust to it.

Grief is our inner or personal response to losing someone or something we love. Grief feels different to different people, and has no measurable time limit or describable quality. It is a natural process of our physical, emotional, and spiritual feelings, not our thoughts. It might be said that grieving comprises the completion of all that has been left undone, within us and with the family and larger community.

Mourning is the outer expression of our grief, the external actions we take to cope with the loss. It shows our sadness, that we miss the person who has died. It provides the opportunity to adjust to our new inner environment and to accept the reality of the loss and change. We may mourn all alone; with our friends and families; through personal, cultural and religious rituals; or not at all.

Relief comes when death ***frees*** a patient from emotional, physical and psychological constraints; ***allows caregivers respite*** from months and even years of worry, anxiety, and hard work; or ***releases*** us from the constant shadow of wondering when the fateful moment will arrive. Since dying and death trigger deep feelings of grief, the "release" aspect of relief is often not honored or given room for expression in our lives. Welcome this bright stranger into your life.

EVERYONE GRIEVES DIFFERENTLY

There is no right or wrong way to grieve and no specific amount of time that it will take. As the loss becomes accepted and integrated into our lives the need to grieve decreases. For example, George grieved for months before the death of his beloved father, Arthur. At Arthur's funeral, George's daughters and wife sobbed but George's eyes were dry. And a California couple states that two years after the sudden and senseless death of their son, they have "finally overcome just enough of their anger to even begin grieving."

The important point is that we may grieve before, during, and after a death, and in the company of others or alone.

LOIS AND THE YA-YA SISTERHOOD

When my mother, Lois, died suddenly, I was so relieved that she went without pain and without lingering in a nursing home—her greatest fear in life—that I actually felt happy. I choked up when the men from the funeral home carried her through the door of her apartment, but soon after I began planning her memorial service and sorting through her belongings. These activities came as a satisfying closure to my physical life with her.

About eight months later, as I was reading "The Divine Secrets of the Ya-Ya Sisterhood," the tears began to flow. I cried for the difficulties in our own mother-daughter relationship. I mourned the lack of any personal connection between Lois and her mother. I grieved the impersonality of the friendships my mother had for so many decades. I knew of countless dinners during which no one ever discussed their feelings, their marriages, or their visions. I wept for mothers and daughters all over the world who couldn't express their feelings to each other, and couldn't support each other's achievements.

I knew it was a good book and many of my friends were reading and enjoying it, but no one seemed to be sobbing like I was. Then I realized it had been the key to unlock the grief I held inside. With every good cry, my heart opened wider to my mother's beauty, her feistiness, her love of the ocean, and how much she accomplished with so few tools offered to her by her mother.

I will forever be grateful to the "Ya-Ya Sisterhood."

WHAT HAPPENS WHEN WE DON'T EXPRESS OR UNDERSTAND OUR GRIEF

When we don't take the time to grieve, repressed emotions including fear, anger, depression, and sadness may interfere with our everyday life. If we don't acknowledge our anxiety, resentment, and guilt, we project them onto other people and situations long after a death has occurred.

The shock of our loss can also lead to physical symptoms, such as sleep disturbance, nightmares, loss of energy, inability to focus at work or school, loss of appetite, restlessness, and unexplained aches and pains.

HELEN: "DOCTOR, I KEEP HAVING THIS PAIN IN MY CHEST."

Helen flew across the country to be with her dying mother Elsie. She spent two months caring for her and trying to make sure she would be able to die at home, honoring Elsie's request.

Helen's father Jack had very different views about

Elsie's care. He was not comfortable watching his wife's physical deterioration—her natural dying process. Also, his insurance would pay more for Elsie to be hospitalized than to have someone care for her at home. Shortly before Helen's work-leave was up, Jack called 911 during the night, hoping to avoid arguing with his daughter. Helen awoke and begged him to rescind the request, to no avail. Elsie, who was peacefully near death, was taken to the hospital where she was rehydrated via IVs and spent her remaining nine days begging to be "taken home."

Helen felt so sorry that she had not helped her mother remain at home, nor could she take time to return for the small family memorial service. She had young children to raise, a husband to care for, and a full time job. Over the following several years Helen lived her everyday life but experienced intermittent chest pains. She went to the doctor. Nothing was physically wrong. Her heart was fine and her lungs worked well. But the pain continued. When Helen returned to the doctor, he asked, "Do you feel like you have a heavy weight on your chest?" When she answered, "Yes, that is exactly the feeling," he asked her if she had undergone a loss recently. She was astounded he should ask and burst into tears. She continued to cry intermittently and unpredictably for weeks. When she finally stopped, the chest pain was gone, never to return.

WHAT KIND OF HELP IS AVAILABLE

Immediately after a death, there are often many chores to take care of, from the funeral to figuring out finances. Once the initial dust has settled, some mourners may be able to determine their own best ways to grieve. They may allow their tears to flow, write in a journal, rest and sleep more than usual, sort through letters and photos, letting memories aid the grief process. Some may also ask for help or participate with others in a variety of ways.

FAMILY, FRIENDS, AND THE PASSAGE OF TIME

Being able to comfortably talk about the loss that is anticipated or has taken place will do a world of good for our own psyches, as well as open doors of connection for those to whom we speak. It helps when we use the "real words"— *dying and death* —rather than euphemisms, such as passed away, which only increase the denial of what is really happening.

Learning from the experiences of others during their grieving may be achieved when we open our hearts and ask, "How did you get through the time following your husband's death?" Also, when we can tell our friends that we are suffering, they can offer resources that benefited them.

Vicky Cromwell shared her experiences after the death of her 19-year-old daughter in her booklet, *Vicky's Testimony of Grief: Suggestions for Helping Each Other.* Some of the most difficult encounters, she reported, were people saying, "God surely has a greater need for her"—something a grieving mother can't fathom—or "Do you have other children?" as if they could take the place of the daughter who had just died.

She offered the following suggestions:

✧   You don't have to say anything, just be there.
✧   Allow the bereaved to speak often of the memories of their loved one.
✧   Acknowledge there was a death rather than pretending all is as it was before.
✧   Offer simple decisions such as "I am having soup at six tonight. Will you join us?"
✧   Allow tears, yours and hers, when you visit.
✧   Realize there is never a day that the loved one is forgotten.
✧   The feelings of sorrow will change.

Simply being quiet in our grief and being quiet as we support someone we love in her grief can bring peace. "A loving silence often has far more power to heal and to connect than the most well intentioned words," says Rachel Naomi Remen in *Kitchen Table Wisdom*.

CULTURAL AND RELIGIOUS CUSTOMS

There are as many rites and rituals for helping us process our grief as there are religions, countries, and ethnic groups. Most of them include the honoring and remembering of the person who has died. This occurs not only at the time of death and during the funeral or memorial but also on specific dates that follow, such as one year from the death, or at specific cultural celebrations that have evolved for this purpose.

Personal Places of Worship

As with birth, clergy participate in the dying process of their congregants. From the first notification of a severe diagnosis, religious leaders offer assistance to the ill person and his family. This includes visiting and counseling with family members, both spiritually–by helping make sense of the impending death, and practically–by assisting with plans for the funeral. When a sudden death occurs, one's spiritual mentor can be extremely helpful in providing guidance. Often, grief support groups are offered before, during and after the death, in addition to individual counseling. Acknowledging and honoring the loss a year later may also be part of the process.

Rabbi Steven Carr Reuben, from Pacific Palisades, California, said, "I usually find myself talking more about funerals than weddings or baby namings, because the opportunity I constantly have as a rabbi to be there for others at the time of their greatest emotional need is a rare privilege."

Day of the Dead (Día de los Muertos)

Every year on November 1, All Saint's Day, and November 2, All Souls' Day, Mexican people gather to remember loved ones who have died. Families create special altars, *ofrendas,* in their homes or at the cemetery. Items placed on the *ofrendas* include reproductions of skulls, coffins, and bones—often formed into candies and cakes—candles, photographs of the deceased, bouquets of marigolds, fruit, and paper flowers. The feast and the colorful symbols are to encourage a visit from the deceased, so they can know that the family continues to honor them. Marigold petals are strewn in bright golden pathways, inviting the dead to see the altar and visit the family. At the same time, the careful consideration put into creating the altar is an act of celebrating life as a way to remember death.

Sitting Shiva

Shiva is a seven-day Jewish ritual following a death to show respect for the deceased and give comfort to the living. There are many variations and customs depending on the Jewish community—some vigorous, some festive. Most often the immediate family members remain in the home, with friends and relatives visiting during the week. Shaving and changing clothes are not allowed. It is traditional for visitors to bring prepared food and sweets to ease the bitterness of loss for the grieving family. Mirrors are covered with white cloth, and a special candle burns for the *Shiva* period. Prayers are recited and stories and remembrances of the person who has died are shared. About a year later the gravestone is placed and unveiled. Family and friends gather for prayers and shared food, while a special candle is lit and burned for 24 hours.

Obon

> Every summer, Japanese Buddhists celebrate *Obon*, The Feast
> of Lanterns. The ceremony honors those who died in the
> past, particularly those during the previous year. Lanterns are
> lit and food is offered to guide the spirits of the ancestors.
> Specially prepared foods are also served to guests and friends,
> creating both a spiritual and joyful occasion. In some
> districts, lighted candles are placed on little floats. The
> gathered people watch them move down a river or out to
> sea, accompanied by special dances and songs.

Irish Wakes

> In the traditional wake, family and friends gather from the
> time of the death until the body leaves for the funeral. It is
> an important part of the grieving process, as comfort is
> offered along with the opportunity to tell stories about the
> deceased. Food, drink, and music are part of celebrating the
> life that has just ended. The deceased is given a send off to
> the next life. At times, women will keen, a lamentation that
> sounds like wailing. The family has immediate help available
> for the tasks of death, as well as the opportunity to feel and
> share the loss.

PROFESSIONAL HELP

> Excellent grief counseling is available, both for people who
> have already experienced a loss and those who are
> anticipating a death because of a diagnosed illness or
> advanced age. Even if a great deal of time has passed since a
> loved one died, grief counseling can still be valuable.

Why do we need the help of professionals when we have families, friends, and clergy willing to assist us? Because grief counselors have been trained to anticipate the many nuances associated with loss and have learned numerous ways to help the bereaved. Their experience of sitting with many mourners brings an expertise greater than most of us will ever gain.

In addition, it is not always easy for people to discuss loss and grief with those closest to them, especially if they hadn't discussed the possibilities of dying and death before a diagnosis was made. For example, a wife who is dying may not be able to express her feelings of fear and anger to her husband since she knows he is already suffering at the news of her diagnosis. The husband may be unwilling to express his feelings because he believes his wife needs only his support. If they see a counselor separately and express and explore their feelings with her, she can then help them sit together and communicate, with her guidance. Thus, they can better understand the ways to be present with each other during this very significant time of their lives.

A GRIEF COUNSELOR'S STORY

I received a telephone call from a distraught widower, the father of three small children. His wife became ill at a picnic and was taken to the nearest hospital. She was not diagnosed correctly and sent to a hospital designated by her health insurance carrier, by which time she was in a coma. She died shortly thereafter, with family present when life-support was disconnected. Not only was there the sudden and tragic loss of their young mother and wife, the family also had a great deal of anger because of the medical errors.

I went to the home and visited with the father and his children. After the funeral the older children, ages six and eight, began attending my children's grief support group. I did one-on-one counseling with the father and assisted him in helping his children to adjust at home to the loss. This included getting household help, as well as creating new . routines and ways of spending time together as a family.

For two years in a row, the entire family attended our holiday memorial gathering where we celebrate the lives of those who have died in the past year, as well as the caregivers and family who are mourning their loss.

The children still attend group, as a way of identifying and coping with their feelings. Although the father was sure he would never find another woman to love, he has. The youngest son, now four, attends a group for younger children that is based on play therapy.

This father says that he could never have gotten through the past two-and-one-half years without the help and support we have provided.

Professional grief counseling can also enhance the dying process. Talking honestly about dying and death helps us deal with the physical, emotional, spiritual, and existential suffering that most encounter when approaching end of life. These conversations allow us to accept what is happening, express the fear of the unknown, and let go with greater ease when the time comes.

When a person or family initiates grief counseling, an "intake appointment" will be scheduled, during which the counselor will gather information to determine the best kind of help to offer. When the situation is complicated, such as described in the previous story, one-on-one work may be suggested, at least for a time.

In most instances, specific support groups will be

suggested in which age and type-of-loss are considered. Group meetings show how others are integrating their losses and creating new lives, decrease the sense of isolation, offer models of expressing inhibited or repressed feelings, and often provide the nucleus of a new community. A group experience will not fit everyone's personality or need, in which case individual counseling may be an effective alternative. Some of the major categories of support groups include:

★   *Loss of a life-partner.* The change in daily life after the loss of a partner is traumatic, but the reasons for the changes can be significantly different: early marriages may include small children, financial commitments, and loss of shared visions; those in long-term marriages may face chronic illness and inexperience with simple domestic tasks that one partner had previously assumed.

★   *Sudden death.* In addition to the loss itself, the shock of sudden death adds extra implications in the grieving process. If one did not witness the death, the imagination can be vivid in creating the dying scenarios. If one viewed a death, which included physical mutilation, the mental replay can run again and again. Also, there has been no preparation or warning of any kind to lead gradually into a grieving process.

★   *Suicide.* The need to "normalize" a suicide is of extra importance. Often the survivor brings guilt, shame, and the "if only I had..." syndrome. In a group they can see that other survivors have learned how suicide is the cause of death from an illness—depression—and not a crime that was "committed."

★   *Children.* It is especially supportive for a child to be part of a group when a parent or sibling is in the dying process. The counselors help the children keep current with their feelings, memorialize the person they are losing, and not to feel "different." Artwork is used extensively for the children to express themselves. Using and hearing the words "dying" and "death" aid their understanding and connect a language to the loss. Often, children continue to benefit from a group long after the death.

★ *Parents who have lost children.* Possibly the greatest loss of all is suffered by parents whose children have died. Those who have recently lost a child gain support from parents who, with time and assistance from others, have healed enough to go on with their lives. The mission of *The Compassionate Friends* is "to assist families toward the positive resolution of grief following the death of a child of any age and to provide information to help others be supportive." This national, non-profit organization has no religious affiliation and no membership dues or fees. See p. 255.

CELEBRATING DEATH AND LOSS AS RELIEF

The previous discussions in this chapter describe assistance for processing grief. However, there are also times when a loss leads directly to relief. With a slight change in perspective, we could be celebrating death more often. Grief will still be a component of the loss, but tempered with acceptance and relief.

The narrative approach to death, dying, and grief

Lorraine Hedtke is a hospice clinical social worker and family therapist. After many years of sitting with the dying and their families, she views death not as finality, but as an invitation to a new relationship with a loved one. Rather than working to "get over" our grief so we can "move on,"

Hedtke suggests telling stories about the person who is dying, or has died, in order to "re-member" them and affirm the ongoing nature of life. She does not assume that people should complete a process of farewell and letting go in order to progress healthily through the crisis of death.

In co-constructing stories of hope and love, with the dying person if possible and with friends and family who come to the bedside of the dying, a celebration of life takes place rather than a focus on his death. Hedtke describes this process in her book, *Re-Membering Lives: Conversations with the Dying and the Bereaved.*

Liberating Losses

Sometimes, death brings relief instead of grief. This can happen after a very long illness and dying process, or when it is known that the deceased had suffered intense pain or anguish. When death leads to the end of an abusive relationship, relief may also be felt. Because feelings of relief, freedom, and independence are not accepted in our traditional view of loss, we have few possibilities for expressing expansive and positive feelings without guilt.

Jennifer Elison and Chris McGonigle experienced such losses. They also interviewed over forty people who described their feelings of relief after losing a close family member or friend. The authors share these stories in *Liberating Losses: When Death Brings Relief.*

HOW TO FIND HELP FOR GRIEF AND THE GRIEVING

While one can find bereavement resources in the yellow pages or by calling local institutions, grief-work is personal and intimate, and best accomplished with someone you trust and are comfortable with. If necessary, interview several prospective counselors until you find just the right person. The most direct way to seek help is by following a known connection, either a person or organization with which you are familiar. The following suggestions are possible ways to begin.

* *Word of Mouth.* Gather information from the personal experiences of those you know and respect. Ask friends and family members for the ways in which they lived their days, weeks, and months during and after the dying process and death of a loved one. If you are witnessing family members or friends grieve, share with them what you learned during your time of bereavement when they are ready to listen.
* *Clergy.* Your own place of worship may offer grief support groups and individual counseling as well as other resources in the community.
* *Hospice.* When a family agrees to receive hospice care, bereavement counseling is included. Knowing this before a crisis occurs provides the benefit of anticipatory grief counseling. This may or may not decrease the pain of the loss, but it allows one to be more present with the one who is dying. Anticipatory grief-work does decrease the intensity of the shock when the death occurs. Fewer regrets, "if onlys," and mysteries persist when the conversations have taken place. Bereavement groups and individual grief counseling are usually available without cost for at least a year, and sometimes longer when needed.
* *Hospitals.* If your loved one died in a hospital and you wish to receive grief counseling, the best place to start is the hospital social worker or the case-manager. She will have local resources available and recommendations for your specific needs.
* *Our House.* For those in the Los Angeles area, Our House welcomes all who seek assistance with grieving. See p. 255.

SEPARATION LEADING TO CONNECTION

In addition to our personal losses, we also grieve those of our country and our world, such as 9/11 and the continued violence between people of many countries and diverse religious faiths. The community resources described above may also be helpful in processing the seemingly senseless deaths over which we have no control. Just as a broken or fragmented family often reconnects in new ways because of a crisis, so may our ability to cope and our outlook shift in supportive and unifying ways when loss occurs due to natural disasters, war, or other forms of human violence.

For many of us, breaking out of old and rigid attitudes and familiar patterns occurs *only* when spurred by external circumstances. Our minds and hearts are broken open. We see larger patterns of connections, relationships, and possibilities. When things appeared one way–the only way–oftentimes a crisis brings a fresh point of view.

Expressing our feelings of loss or relief helps us remain, or become, connected to our families, our friends, and ourselves. Everyone suffers loss. Each of us must learn how to heal, make sense of our loss, and continue living and loving. This path is softened by the loving presence of others.

aindrops roll like tears

Along the green shiny leaf

Pushed by warm sun rays

C. W.

PART III

Putting Facts and Feelings into Action:

Exercises and Action Steps

Integrating into our lives the information, points of view, and personal experiences of Part II.

Thirteen

Explore Your Feelings

*Why is it easier to express grief
for an English princess in a French tunnel
than it is to visit a dying neighbor down the block?*

—— Nancy Cobb, *In Lieu of Flowers: A Conversation for the Living*

AFRAID, MAD, SAD, AND GLAD

In addition to cultural taboos, and decades of social habits and
manners, our feelings—represented by fear, anger, sadness,
happiness—most often keep us from facing the final mystery.

Fear is probably the strongest feeling associated with dying and
death. None of us know what death is like; we have not yet died.
The unknown—death—is always surrounded with fear, real and
imagined. If we can name the fears and understand the role they play
in our lives, we can then learn to accept and work with them. Fear
definitely does not disappear by ignoring it. It goes underground to
some part of our psyche and keeps us from being fully present. It
may lead us to say, "I don't want to talk about those awful subjects,"

or prevent us from spending time with loved ones who need care and succor. This hidden fear is not serving a useful role in our lives.

Anger often follows in the footsteps of fear. When we are faced with the unknown, we feel out of control. The most immediate reaction to lack of control is anger.

LORRAINE'S MISPLACED ANGER

Lorraine's father was diagnosed with advanced, untreatable lung cancer. She flew into a rage at his doctors for their failure to help him. She accused them of doing the wrong tests and not providing the right treatment.

There could be many possible explanations for her rage. It temporarily protected her from feeling the impending loss of her father. It spared her the self-examination of her own smoking habit and its obvious health risks. It deflected anger directed at her father for smoking all his adult life.

Although these feelings may seem irrational, they are quite real and can interfere with the intimacy she could be experiencing with her family during this crisis.

Sadness can also keep us from facing death. We don't want to lose people we love. We don't want to leave this beautiful planet through our own death. Americans are "happy hungry" folks. Self-help books and seminars, diets, clothes, cigarettes and booze promise us happiness as quickly as possible. By not embracing and experiencing the grief from previous losses, we prevent ourselves from being present for the transitions and changes we must all endure in the future.

Happiness, too, may be an ally that contributes to our avoidance of discussing end-of-life issues. Why interrupt a lively dinner party with "morbid conversation?" Why darken a sunny day with talk of death? On the other hand, how do we learn to be comfortable saying "I'm glad…" instead of sad when someone we know dies? We don't have a socially acceptable way of speaking our relief.

THE SHADOW

In a *Los Angeles Times* Book Section, the titles or descriptions of eleven of the fifteen fiction bestsellers included the words, murder, killing, mayhem, death, dying, or homicide. We don't want to talk about the dying and death that will occur within our own families, although it seems that the general population is very eager to read about it as fiction or watch media violence. Does becoming absorbed in a detective novel keep the dying "out there" and allow our denial to continue? The focus on the deaths of public figures such as Princess Diana and John Kennedy, Jr. also keeps tragedy in some other family, and prevents the personal examination of our own mortality.

We all tend to rally when natural or political disasters of great magnitude occur. If they are in a foreign country, we donate money to the Red Cross. If they are local, we give time and effort to help those affected. Can we embrace the enormity of losses that we will all suffer, and still function and have compassion? Can feeling the losses of others help us prepare for our own? How can we "participate joyfully in the sorrows of the world," as Joseph Campbell suggested?

The following exercises will help you consider the contents of your "big bag"—your unacknowledged and unexpressed emotions—and help release energy to become available for focused relationships, including discussing dying and death, creativity, good health, and the ability to care for ourselves and others in need.

EXERCISES

Note: Each of these exercises may be enhanced by referring to the **ACTION STEPS** at the end of the chapters.

FEELING, NOT THINKING

The purpose of this exercise is to see that repressed feelings prevent us from accomplishing necessary tasks; that sharing our feelings connects us to one another; and most significantly, that we can create the opportunity for expanding the community we need to care for one another.

Gather three or four friends or family members together. Tell them you are interested in hearing what their feelings are about their own mortality and that of their loved ones. Explain that you are using this book to examine your own situation and that they can help you, as well as begin their own explorations.

Begin by asking each person to tell a personal incident related to dying and death. Everyone has at least one story. Usually, the first person's story elicits commonalties, questions, and feelings that can then be shared. If someone is shy, let him pass on his turn. He will learn by listening and may want to participate later.

If the story has focused only on the "facts," gently ask questions of each other as to how a certain event or situation made them feel, and what those feelings may have prevented in the way of interacting with others during the situation.

Allow approximately 45 minutes for this sharing to take place. Discuss what feelings were evoked and if any shifts in attitude had taken place. Typically, attitudes change by learning that the "private" feelings, once made "public," are similar to others in the group.

Suggest that each participant make a list of three steps

to take in the following week as a result of this exercise.

Make a plan to meet again in a few weeks to share how this session was used within families or with other friends, and what tasks were accomplished.

WRITING WITHOUT EDITING

The purpose here is to allow stream-of-consciousness writing to override normal busy thought patterns, allowing feelings and new ideas to surface.

Find a tranquil place to sit, bring a pen or pencil and a tablet of writing paper. If you are a meditator, use your own techniques to settle your mind. If not, some simple stretches and deep, repetitive breathing can help create a peaceful and quiet atmosphere. Classical music also induces relaxation.

Begin by thinking of the conversations you may have been attempting to have with family members concerning dying and death. Think of situations that you have witnessed that have been unsatisfactory. Think of movies or books that have aroused your interest in dying and death or made you wonder about these issues in your own life.

Start writing whatever comes to mind. Write what you think might happen if you bring up certain topics. Travel mentally to each of the people you care about that has a need to face end-of-life issues in some way, including yourself. Keep writing whatever comes into your mind without censoring your thoughts. Do not edit your writing style. Do not imagine what anyone else will say if they were to find this tablet. No one else will read this. Spend at least 20-30 minutes writing and then rest.

Reread what you have written and with highlighter pen, mark places where you can see emotions that either enhanced or inhibited a scenario. Label certain situations with anger, fear, sadness, joy, or guilt to bring clarity to what emotions lay behind the interactions.

Begin thinking of the steps you can take to deal with these feelings, whether it be forging ahead anyway, learning more communication skills, or even seeking counseling.

Write down three steps to take in the next week to begin your journey of exploring your feelings around living, dying, and death.

EXPRESSING FEELINGS THROUGH ART

This third exercise leads to feelings and thoughts that are non-linear, or haven't yet moved themselves into words.

If you have time to do this exercise immediately after either previous exercise, you may be able to translate your accessed feelings directly into art. You may want to do this with several friends or family members, after the writing exercise. However, this can be done easily on your own.

Gather any art supplies you have, including crayons, colored pencils, pastels, and watercolors. Find colored construction paper, as colors often provide information about feelings that we don't know we have. Sometimes black paper evokes nothingness and allows buried feelings to emerge from bright pastel crayons. Include scissors, tape, paste, and images from old magazines. Also, clay can be a wonderful tool for fashioning hidden thoughts and feelings into form.

Important: Before lifting a finger or a crayon, suspend the belief that "you are not an artist" and that you "can't even draw a straight line." This is not about craft, quality or talent, but about expression. (Remember how you or your children could draw pleasurably and meaningfully for hours, until someone criticized the work.)

Once you feel quiet, take several deep breaths and approach the art supplies. Begin. Delete judgment. Forget your marketing list. Just draw or paint or sculpt.

If you are doing this exercise with some friends, share any ideas that appear to you after you have looked at the art piece. If you are alone, or if you can't yet see anything new in your drawing, tape it on the refrigerator and look at it for a few days until it speaks to you. Describing your insights out loud can often bring even more information that you couldn't see until you gave voice to it, in the same way that telling a dream out loud can amplify its meaning.

A SIMPLE PARADOX

One workshop participant, a very "left-brain lawyer," drew a line that started in one corner of the page and continued in circles until it ended in a dot at the center of the page. He began describing it to the group as his "image of life," getting smaller and smaller until death. Then he held the drawing in front of himself and suddenly saw its reverse. Startled, he said, "What if life starts at the little dot in the center and circles out, growing wider and wider, more and more expansive, until one can soar out of it?"

EXPLORING FEELINGS THROUGH POETRY

Maya Angelou said, "Poetry is music written for the human heart." Poetry, like painting, can reach into the areas of the brain that are not so rational, the areas that feel, instead of think. Creating poetry can do the same, as long as you don't hold judgment over your results. A poem can be complete with a beginning, middle and end, or it can be a succession of words that attach feelings to metaphors. It can rhyme or not rhyme. It can have form or be formless.

In my workshops, I have found the structured form of traditional Haiku poetry appeals to many that are unpracticed at writing poetry. However, your expression need not adhere to this rigid format, and you may break any of its rules.

Haiku guidelines...

Write three lines.

* The first, of five syllables...
  relating to some form of nature
* The second, of seven syllables...
  indicating an action
* The third, again of five syllables...
  renaming the subject in the first

Red leaves of plum tree
Curl up and lose their shine
Falling in autumn

If you are doing this exercise with friends or family, share the results out loud. Listen for nuances of feeling or meaning that you couldn't see or hear while you were writing.

Enjoy this exercise!

Participants at Facing the Final Mystery workshops wrote all of the poems that appear at the end of each chapter.

KEEPING A JOURNAL

Now you may continue your inner dialogue concerning the most intimate and pertinent questions you are (or will be) facing.

Writing down feelings, thoughts, and ideas in a journal can be valuable in all aspects of life. This is unexpectedly true with the deeply held feelings surrounding dying and death. In my workshops, I have seen how writing a series of questions is a stimulating way to begin the process. Create your own, or use the following questions to get started.

Use either a separate journal for exploring your end-of-life issues or continue this process in a journal that you are already using.

★   What feelings do I have when I imagine my own death?

★   Describe how I imagine my dying process and how that makes me feel.

★   What feelings do I have as I watch my own aging process?

★   What feelings arise within me when a conversation relating to dying and death takes place?

★   What situations related to dying and death created feelings of guilt in me?

★   What dying and death experiences have led me to feelings of relief, release, and joy?

★   Describe my feelings the last time I learned that a loved one died.

★   If I have received a serious diagnosis, how did I feel when I heard the news? Or when I shared the information with a friend or family member for the first time?

While a journal is usually a private experience, this exercise offers several benefits for sharing the results with others. The questions may create an easier transition to conversation with family members. Learning about the feelings of others close to you can bring support as we face the final mystery.

ACTION STEPS

1. Record a list of the incidents in which you feel angry, sad, afraid, or happy that do not seem directly related to the situation at hand.

2. Read *Kitchen Table Wisdom* by Rachel Naomi Remen. See p. 256.

3. Record your night dreams. Describe them with art materials.

4. Watch the video called *Antonia's Line*. See p. 241.

5. Write a poem.

6. Buy a blank book to use as a journal.

7. If you like doing the "Writing Without Editing" exercise, read *The Artist's Way* by Julia Cameron, for more detailed descriptions of how to incorporate these "morning pages" into your daily routine. See p. 239.

Life is in the wind

The wind caresses the leaf

That dry, falls to earth

D.B.

Fourteen

Listen to Stories

This packrat has learned that what the next generation will value most is not what we owned, but the evidence of who we were and the tales of how we loved. In the end, it's the family stories that are worth the storage.

— Ellen Goodman, *Boston Globe*

HOW STORIES HELP

We all know people who have important stories to tell, yet many who have suffered the loss of a loved one feel their stories would burden others. Lifting the taboos of talking about dying and death increases our comfort so that we can ask family and friends to share their most important times of achievement and loss. We benefit from hearing their stories and we learn new ways to help others go through their losses. An often, unrecognized benefit is that telling the story helps to heal the storyteller. In fact, even if the telling of them releases tears and difficult memories, it also releases stored pain and the loneliness of carrying the memory without help.

In his book, *The Wisdom of Dying*, N. Michael Murphy, MD, describes the value of telling stories from his work with hospice patients. He says, "The dying storyteller is oftentimes literally more free in his breathing—and able to expire in peace—after recounting tales of his roots and a few of the joys and pains that went along with them." He also reports how a patient's physical pain would often diminish after telling a story and having it witnessed by family.

If telling stories on the deathbed can help release the physical body, telling the stories earlier may help ease the fear with which many approach death, or even the thought of death. There is also the chance that learning each other's stories will enrich the relationships we now have with one another.

Tuesdays With Morrie

Since 1997, our country has been listening to the story of a wise old man named Morrie Schwartz. He contracts a slowly debilitating disease and decides to pay attention to every facet of his remaining time. A friend sent Morrie's collection of aphorisms—such as "Accept what you are able to do and what you are not able to do," and "Learn to forgive yourself and forgive others"—to a reporter at the *Boston Globe*. Ted Koppel, from television's *Nightline* program, became intrigued with the story headline, "A Professor's Final Course: His Own Death," and made arrangements to interview Morrie.

When Mitch Albom saw Morrie, his former, beloved college professor, being interviewed by Ted Koppel, he contacted him and began visiting each Tuesday afternoon until Morrie's death. Mr. Albom was willing and eager to listen. Because he listened—and wrote—we all have the benefit of his story, as told in *Tuesdays with Morrie: An Old Man, a Young Man, and Life's Greatest Lesson*. The book has also been made into audiotapes read by the author, as well as a movie for television produced by Oprah Winfrey.

Mitch and Morrie discussed specific topics each week, including death, the family, emotions, fear of aging, money, love, and the world. As the discussions progressed, Morrie declined physically, requiring increased levels of care, yet his mind remained clear and he continued to teach. Albom concludes that the most important lesson of all was: "There is no such thing as 'too late' in life. Morrie was changing until the day he said good-bye."

After listening to Morrie's story and wisdom, one is compelled to ask, "Whom can I listen to now? Whom can I talk to now?"

JOHANNES IN DENMARK

During my father's 92nd summer I took him on a two-week trip to his homeland, Denmark. He had said almost daily that he wanted to make another trip there. Most of my friends felt Johannes was too old to travel and it would be too hard on me. Some of my elderly massage clients even suggested I take him to Solvang (a Danish village in Southern California), saying he wouldn't know the difference! But his persistence pushed me to make the arrangements.

We made it through the airplanes and airports—it wasn't easy—and settled into our relatives' homes. His current memory, which is normally poor, became almost nonexistent for several days. I thought I had made a big mistake. Slowly, as he saw the Danish signs and heard the language being spoken, his ancient memories were stimulated and shared. I watched as our cousins looked up to him in admiration, and provided generous hospitality—pastries fresh from a local baker each morning, open-faced sandwiches and akavit for lunch. My father sat and smiled, ate and drank, and answered questions. He was the only one of his generation who was still alive. Though he had left

Denmark when he was 21, he still had a clear memory of the landscape, the language, and the relationships between his family and the villagers. I burst into tears every few hours as I watched these people know my father, give him back his status in the world, give him back his history. In Los Angeles, every one of his friends had died, as well as my mother, his wife of 63 years. His poor memory prevented the making of new friends. But in his past he shone, the elder, the storyteller.

Not only was this trip a fulfillment for him—we looked at the photographs and talked about each part of the journey during our weekly visits—it was especially important to Else, one of my cousins who was undergoing a recurrence of cancer. She took special time with my father, encouraging me to go off with my younger cousins. Else reported that when he began repeating a story, she merely asked him a different question about a different time or place, and he would go right there. (This taught me a new way to listen and participate in his often-repeated memories.) She learned detailed vignettes about her father—his brother—that she had never heard before. Else had no other elder to question and gather her own early history as she moved toward her untimely death. When I think of our trip now, I sometimes feel the journey was more for Else than for my dad. We all listened to each other.

LOIS IN GREATER LOS ANGELES

During the last year of my mother's life, she asked if I would accompany her and my father on a tour of the homes she had lived in throughout her life. She was not ill, but at 86 she thought her end might be near, and she was tying up loose ends.

We began our journey on a Sunday morning with my grown son at the wheel. We stopped in Inglewood to see the first home they had built and where they had lived when I was born. We were able to peek down the driveway and see the large stone barbecue they had built from rocks they had gathered during trips to the desert. The current owners came out and my parents told them what the neighborhood was like when they arrived in 1937. Next, we stopped in front of a blue apartment building facing an old fashioned central court, to which they had returned from their honeymoon on Catalina Island.

Continuing east, we stopped at the collection of now ramshackle houses my grandfather built in Lincoln Heights, where my mother had lived from the moment she was born in 1910 until she married. Gone were the white paint on the walls, the green lawns, and the leaded window panels that had lined the front porch. But the memories remained and came forth, as my son and I asked questions and listened to the details that comprised her young life. I had lived in one of the apartments as a child and had my own memories that my parents now amplified for me. My son had never been there, nor to any of the parts of Los Angeles through which we were traveling. In addition to participating in his grandmother's dream, he was getting history and geography lessons.

Nearby was the church where my parents were married. I had never seen it except in photographs. We stopped at the corner that had once held the laundry where my parents met, and heard how my mother had spotted my tall handsome father when he brought his three shirts in every three days.

We made two more stops in Highland Park and Eagle Rock, where I had grown up, and finally had dinner at Taix's restaurant in Silver Lake. From my infancy until I left home for college, we had often dined as a family in its former location near Union Station. My son and I are both grateful for this day. I also feel quite certain that it helped my mother prepare for her death the following winter.

EXERCISES

RECORD A LIFE STORY

Many have sensed the value of gathering the stories of elders. As a result, there are businesses that record them on audio and videotapes, and more recently, CDs. If you don't feel you know what to ask, or have the equipment to record, consult your local church or temple for professional life-story recorders. Also visit the Association for Personal Historians. See p. 237.

Conducting the conversations on your own will bring the greatest rewards to both parties. Here are some practical guidelines:

★ Prepare a list of questions to guide the story. See p. 282.

★ Here are some general areas of interest: a chronology of significant life events; a list of interests, skills, insights, ancestors and kin; education; life at home and at work.

★ What specifically do you want to know about the storyteller? The answers will guide your questioning.

★ Allow two to four hours to conduct the interview. You may want to do it in several sessions, breaking it down into certain eras or topics.

★ Let the storyteller know you are interested in *all* parts of their life, not just the happy moments.

★ Assure them you are especially curious about any difficult or troubling parts of their lives, such as family secrets or feelings of guilt, and that you will not judge them for the past. Let them know how healing it can be to allow the private stories to come forth and be witnessed.

★ Help them to understand the benefit it will be to you to know your own ancestors and histories.

★ Once you ask the questions, listen. Don't judge or criticize.

★ If the answers are brief, ask additional questions to ellicit more details.

★ Once the stories have been collected, you may edit them, omitting repetitions or unwanted sounds.

★ Consider making gifts to other family members of audio or videotapes of your elders.

★ Begin thinking of the stories you want to share with your descendents.

★ Remember that stories heal both the teller and the listener.

★ Enjoy this process.

LIVING EXPRESSIONS

"Living Expressions" are formal events where friends and relatives gather together to purposefully share appreciative feelings to a living recipient. The event may take place on the recipient's birthday or held on any occasion. The idea is based upon the eulogy at which appreciative feelings are spoken and witnessed by friends and family of a person who has died. Pash Galbavy and Marty Landa pursued the idea of offering a eulogy to someone who is alive.

The event provides the opportunity to express love and appreciation to one another. Depending on the number of participants, this can take several hours or an entire weekend. Such gatherings include opportunities to disclose feelings that are not necessarily positive as long as they are expressed in the context of love and appreciation. For example, a daughter describing how criticized she felt as a teenager, but how she now sees the benefits she received during that time.

Many hospice caregivers report that patients who seem past the point of physically living, hang on until they are able to express love or forgiveness to a family member. Thus, the importance of these expressions, before a loved one has died, becomes a gift for all involved.

To create your own Living Expressions event, invite family members and friends to your celebration. Ask them to be prepared to describe the effect the recipient has had on their life, and to express appreciation about the qualities and accomplishments of the recipient. Make it a festive occasion!

ACTION STEPS

1. Make a list of people you love whose stories you have never heard.

2. Set time aside to visit and ask questions of those loved ones.

3. Ask your own children what they might like to know about you but have been "afraid to ask."

4. Think of people that you know who have been caretakers for the dying and set time aside to ask for their personal experiences.

5. If you know people who are ill, old, or dying, spend time with them and encourage them to tell you stories about their lives. This might be especially rewarding if you missed

hearing the stories of your own ancestors.

6.   If you are not living near an elderly relative or friend, visit a local nursing home and find a resident to interview, especially one who never receives visitors.

7.   Listen to lectures or tapes presented by those who have studied death and dying, such as Sogyal Rinpoche or Ram Dass. See p. 231

8.   Read any of the books listed under PERSONAL STORIES. See p. 261.

9.   Read, watch or listen to *Tuesdays with Morrie.* See p. 261.

10. Rent and watch the video, *Afterlife.* See p. 240.

Mothers and Daughters

I have one, but not the other

Too soon neither

Aging scares me

My mother's and mine

It is not the silver strands or the little lines that belie the years

The blessings are many hued and rich

But at this moment the losses overwhelm me

The ones that never were and the ones to come.

S.R.

Fifteen

Communicate
Your Wishes, Fears, Hopes,
and Dreams

*The best way to help achieve a comfortable death is low-tech
and old-fashioned, though not simple: conversation.*
—— Denise Grady, *New York Times, 1999*

LET'S TALK NOW

The central purpose of this book is to create comfort in talking
about dying and death. When we exclude discussions relating to
end-of-life issues, we may be removing the glue that can connect
daily life with purpose, intimacy with relationships, health with
awareness. Communication is not just saying words or hearing
words. It is the exchange of feelings, caring acts, personal
information, and shared experiences. It is the way we love.

In this chapter, exercises, resources, and ideas are presented to stimulate new ways of having conversations with loved ones. The suggestions can be done alone or with friends gathering informally, or you might want to create your own workshop setting.

If you are reading this book, you may be the family member who sees the need to take the necessary steps in helping a loved one prepare for dying and death. Yet this worthy plan is not always met with open arms. "We need to talk about end-of-life issues," may garner any one of the following responses:

★ "You make me feel like you want me to die."
★ "I'm not ready to die and I'll let you know when I am."
★ "Are you telling me I'm old and you don't want me around anymore?"
★ "I'm afraid to die. All my friends are dying and I don't want to talk about it."
★ "Let's talk about life instead."
★ "Do you know something about my diagnosis that I don't? I thought they said I'm getting better."
★ "Are you telling me I need to worry about all this now and then worry again later when the real situation occurs?"

SOME WAYS TO BEGIN CONVERSATIONS

Following are some potential and common scenarios to read. You may want to replace them with your specific situation and practice with a friend before trying it with a parent or someone who is ill. Try keeping the conversations based on your needs, beginning with the word "I" as illustrated below. This reduces the sense that you are being critical.

1.   If it is your parents and they are still well and living active lives, try telling a real-life story to illustrate your needs, rather than demanding that they take specific steps.

"Mom and Dad, ever since my friend died last summer at the age of 37, I have become aware that we never know when we will die and that it makes sense to prepare for it ahead of time, as we would for any important event in life. I've been thinking about all of the decisions she had to make in such a short time, when she was feeling so sick and was so scared. So I have made a list of all of my wishes that I know of at this time, and I want to share them with you. I'd like to know what your wishes are, and how I can help you when the time comes if I am still alive. And if I am not, who else would you like to have attend to these matters?"

2. If it is your parents and one or the other of them is ill, either physically or mentally, let them know what your needs are, while still being encouraging and supportive.

   "Mom, Dad, I can see that you aren't feeling as well (thinking as clearly, able to move around as quickly) as you were last year at this time. I'm sure if you keep doing what your doctor tells you (exercising, eating well) you will feel better, but I'd like to talk about what we need to know if either you or Dad gets worse. I want you to make the decisions that are important while you can, so I don't have to wonder and guess at what you wanted. Can you imagine how I'd feel if I had to make a decision about your medical care or your finances and didn't know what you wanted?"

3. If it is a parent, sibling or friend with a serious diagnosis, try offering help along with expressing your needs.

   "I can see you are doing a great job tolerating these treatments. I am here to help you feel the best you can with whatever you need if I feel I can do it. I also want to know if you have any written instructions about how you want things handled, if you are unable to speak for yourself. Things like your desires for continued treatments, when enough is enough, your financial situation, who you want to help you make these decisions. I would like to offer support in every way I can.

4.   If it is you with a serious diagnosis and your loved ones are telling you to stop talking about dying because you're going to get well, remember that honesty is in your best interest, as it is for your friends.

> *"Look, I am going to do everything I can to heal myself and my intention is to get well. But I am very clear, since my diagnosis, that we are all closer to death than I ever thought about before. I want to prepare myself and you, now, whether this illness causes my death or something else causes it 20 years down the line. Here is what I want you to know."*

5.   If it is a loved one who says he is afraid of death, the dying process, or what happens afterward, and just doesn't want to talk about it, offer to help gather information for him.

> *"I can understand that you feel frightened about dying. I think if we begin to find out how other people have dealt with their fears, that maybe we can all be more comfortable with making the plans and decisions that will help us. There is a lot to be learned from books, organizations, and other people's stories. How about if we explore this together, since I need this knowledge too. Then we can talk more freely and get the tasks done."*

EXERCISES

CREATING A CONNECTION

> In her excellent book, *Facing Death and Finding Hope*, Christine Longaker writes about the importance of communication during the end-of-life period. She states: "We've all experienced genuine connection with others

in the past. I always encourage family members to remember a satisfying communication they have had, and to reflect on the qualities which made it go well, which they can draw on once again." These qualities are likely to include:

★ Openness without expectations
★ Really listening to and getting to know the other person
★ A sense of play, an easy humor
★ A sincere willingness to reveal oneself

She goes on to say, "The key is to be natural and to speak from the heart and that we must learn to let go of old positions and fears so that we can spark a change in the relationship."

If communication is important during the dying period, can we begin these conversations now to create connections while we are well, or at least before our loved ones lose the ability to communicate easily?

Using the guidelines above, initiate a conversation with a family member. Make a list of items you want to discuss and information you need to gather.

THE WAY OF COUNCIL

Council is an ancient practice of communication, drawn from many cultures, including Native American, Tibetan, and Quaker. In this practice one person speaks at a time, while everyone else listens intently. The group usually sits in a circle. Some cultures use a "talking piece" to identify the speaker.

Council is an ideal way to talk about end-of-life issues. The normal way of "talking over" one another or shouting louder to be heard can be overcome by using a council format. Its ceremonial flavor relates perfectly to a life passage as important as death. Council allows those who don't want to speak to remain silent and provides the possibility of listening to different points of view without interruption.

Following are situations in which council can be beneficial for facing the final mystery:

★   When feelings are out of control from the fear and upset of a new diagnosis
★   When there is a need for information to be communicated that some family members don't want to hear
★   When there is a need for decisions to be made and a consensus among family members to be reached
★   When there is a need to express love or forgiveness before witnesses within a family
★   When a family member has died and there is a need to verbally share grief

The Way of Council, by Jack Zimmerman and Virginia Coyle, provides the following guidelines. The authors have been leading councils at the Ojai Foundation in California for many years and are currently training groups all over the country to lead councils in public schools, corporations, and other organizations.

PREPARING FOR A COUNCIL

★   Create a setting for a *circle*, even if there will only be two or three present. Being able to see each other clearly is important. If you wished someone to be present who can't (or won't) attend, a pillow or empty chair can be placed in the circle as a reminder of her presence.

★ The *place* can be indoor or outside.

★ Create a *ceremonial environment* by placing something meaningful in the center. This can be a bouquet of flowers, a beautiful rock, crystal, or sculpture. Lighting a candle can signal the beginning of the council. (If ceremony or ritual seems "too much," omit this part—create an environment that feels appropriate to your circle.)

★ The *talking piece* can be as simple as a branch, flower, or shell, or be highly and symbolically decorated. If you or your family have never participated in a council, keep it simple and use a familiar item, such as a family heirloom.

★ Express the need for *confidentiality.*

★ Once you have created the setting, explain the *purpose* and the *method* of the council. Speak only when holding the talking piece—no interrupting or cross talk; you may pass on your turn if you don't want to speak; speak from the heart; listen from the heart; be brief and spontaneous.

★ Next, start the council by posing a question. The first round might address any questions the participants have regarding the council itself. In the case of end-of-life issues, you might include what prevents you from discussing dying and death, what your wishes are for end-of-life care, and how you can help each other during this time of life.

★ After each person has had a turn, offer the opportunity for anyone who has passed to address the first question. When that is completed, pose a second question and pass the talking stick again. Or, the talking stick may be placed in the center of the circle for anyone to pick up and continue the dialogue.

★   Make plans to meet again before you part. Set a time and a topic.

ROLE-PLAYING

Role-playing is another useful tool to practice conversations. This means that you will assume the role of a particular family member (or assign that role to another) for the purpose of learning a new way to understand and deal with a chronic problem. Everyone's goal is to gain new insights into an old dilemma or family drama, by seeing how another person might respond differently as they play you, or some other family member.

Some guidelines for role-playing:

★   First, select a situation that is happening in your life.

★   Then, assign roles to those willing to play, of the main characters in the drama. For example, if you can not get your mother to discuss her end-of-life needs, assign a person to play your mother and another to play you.

★   Describe the problem that you want to work on and give as much background as you can to make the situation seem real.

★   Define roles clearly. Describe the character and some of her characteristics to the person who will be assuming that role. For example, how is your mother likely to respond or resist to or the person who will play her?

★   Have a talker, who will begin acting out the scene; a listener, who will respond to the talker; and an observer, who will watch for physical responses and listen for emotional elements of the dialogue as it takes place.

★ Demonstrate how it works, especially if participants have never done role-playing.

★ Suggest the listener be a "devil's advocate," pushing for numerous responses to the situation.

★ Encourage the observer to keep the dialogue focused, and not allow the participants to wander away from the topic.

ACTION STEPS

1. Initiate one conversation with a peer—someone who is in the same age category and similar life situation—to begin sharing and comparing viewpoints, fears, and experiences.

2. Begin conversing with your parents, if you haven't already done so, ascertaining their needs and desires regarding end-of-life issues.

3. Begin conversations with your children about your potential dying and death.

4. At your next medical appointment, ask your doctor about his feelings regarding end-of-life care. Tell him yours. Tell him you want him to have a copy of your advance directives in your chart.

5. Talk to your clergy person about her points of view and beliefs of death and the afterlife. Ask her to help you with questions or concerns that you have.

6. Read *The Way of Council* in preparation for family conversations, especially if there has been discord or different opinions between family members.

7. Create your own workshop with friends and family using the exercises in this book.

8.   Make a list of any estranged family members or friends that
        you would like to see or talk to again.

9.   Call or write to one of them, expressing your desire to
        reconnect, to apologize or to forgive.

★
★   ★
★

*T*oo late to be felt

Love, the gift, can be withheld

Open, feel the warmth.

D.B.

Sixteen

Create a Team

We live and prosper, sicken and die, too much alone. Families get smaller;
spouses separate, move, and change careers—we all know how it is..

—— Dr. Sukie Miller, introduction to *Share the Care*

WHAT IS A TEAM?

Our methods of providing care for each other have changed a great
deal over the last fifty years. When people move away from their
families and their original communities or get divorced, there begins
the slow attrition of needed support. Whom do we turn to when a
medical crisis happens, when long-term care is needed, or when
major changes occur in our greater community that require the help
of a large number of people?

In this chapter, we will discuss the need for creating new
sources of support, exploring existing circles for potential caregiving,
and locating resources that can assist us in creating new teams. We
will consider both the people who require care, as well as the
providers of that support.

WHEN YOU, OR A LOVED ONE, NEED HELP

If you were to receive a serious medical diagnosis, who will be able to take time off work to help you get to appointments or treatments? Who will look after your children or pets? Who will take care of paying bills or watering the garden? Will you need extra financial support and, if so, to whom might you turn? Who will provide emotional support? Who will become your advocate in the hospital to make sure you are getting the proper care? Where and how will you live if you can't take care of yourself?

If someone you know becomes ill, are you willing to donate time for this person's well being? What are the particular talents or abilities that you can contribute to a team for another's care?

WHEN GIVING CARE IS WEARING YOU DOWN

As often happens when a crisis occurs, one or two people carry the burden of assisting a loved one. This is time-consuming, often exhausting, and may lead to stress, as well as isolation from the community.

Short-term help. Imagine that it is now the fourth week of your friend's chemotherapy treatments. You have driven her to each one and stayed overnight, in addition to shopping for groceries and preparing food for her. Your own work and bills are piling up. You know there is an end in sight, so you figure that you can keep up this pace for a few more months. But can you ask others for help? And if so, what is the best way to approach them?

Long-term help. Consider your mother's need to be driven to doctor's appointments, and keep her flowers blooming. She can't drive now and she can't walk safely on the sloping hillside of her garden, but she could live another twenty years. What are alternative ways to provide care for her over the long haul?

Emergency help. If a sister is in an automobile accident with severe injuries, and her prognosis is unknown, the immediacy and shock of the situation may make it difficult to gather help for her children and her home. Do you even know who her friends are? The organizations she belongs to? Who will oversee her care if you live in another state and have your own children to attend to? How would you go about organizing her care?

Natural and political disasters. In addition to the "normal" upheavals caused by aging, illness and death, we have earthquakes, tornadoes, floods, and, in recent years, terrorist activities, all having a sudden impact with no time for preparation. Injuries, unexpected death, loss of property and jobs can isolate us further from one another.

How could the investment of a small amount of time now set the stage for a smooth transition into responding to such disruptions?

EXPANDING OUR CIRCLES OF MUTUAL AID

We need to develop new ways of living together and caring for each other. Now is the time to create the relationships or teams needed not only for medical emergencies, but also to help each other go through the major changes and crises in our lives, including our aging process and ultimately our dying.

The desire to remain in one's home, alone, until the end, may not be practical or safe if there are no family members living nearby to help. Women outlive men and often continue to live alone for many years after their husbands have died. Aging adults living alone without their longtime mates are often at odds with the simplest housekeeping tasks. Creating a team now while we are still mentally alert and physically capable will reduce the fears associated with aging and dying. This will often reduce the unacknowledged stresses that are already being put on family members. We can begin now to build a new climate of community and create teams to call on in times of need.

WHO IS YOUR TEAM?

A team can be any circle of family, friends, or acquaintances that has an agreement to help one another in the event of a crisis. The qualifications and responsibilities that members will ultimately contribute do not need to be in place at the onset of forming the team. That level of organization will take place when a critical event rallies their participation. What is important is to discuss the concept that we will have a circle of support to turn to in time of crisis.

Preparing to meet

> In order to present the potential impact on the personal lives of your team as it is forming, remind them of the following:
>
> ✧   Extended families are rarely present for each other geographically.
> ✧   Each of us will face illness, aging, dying and death.
> ✧   Illness is not only physical, but also emotional, psychological, spiritual and financial. Therefore, many levels of support will be required.
> ✧   We don't know ahead of time what kind of crisis will befall us, how long it will last, or the kinds of care it will require.
> ✧   A team consisting of people from diverse backgrounds and with multiple talents will improve upon the resources of your extended family.

Explore existing circles for teammates

> Most of us have affiliations with one or more groups of people. These might include a church, book or therapy group, a men's or women's circle, social or special interest club, service organization, exercise class, or school. Within these associations lie relationships that have already been

formed. Some knowledge of each other has been exchanged. Some layers of interest are already in place.

The following are suggestions for building your circle of teammates.

✧   Make a list of the circles you belong to. You might even make a drawing of circles and see where some members overlap.
✧   Decide if you want to address your entire existing group or just selected members.
✧   Develop a list of points to discuss. *(See "Preparing to meet" above.)*
✧   Contact the potential participants from your existing groups, family members, and good friends for a meeting to discuss forming a support team.
✧   Invite them to a potluck so that your first meeting will be a festive event for the exchange of information and ideas.

The nuts and bolts of team building

Imagine what it would be like if a natural or political disaster took place and well-known "teams" such as the Red Cross or FEMA did not already exist. To create such organizations *after* the disaster occurred could be compared to creating your personal team from scratch, *after* severe diagnosis is made for you or a loved one. Following are some essential points to share and tasks to accomplish:

✧   Select a leader and a coordinator
✧   Create a roster that includes all pertinent information for each team member: phone, email, and address; possible health issues; blood type; names and phone numbers of doctors, family, and friends that should be

called in event of an emergency.

✧ Determine how and where this list can be conspicuously available in each household.

✧ Name a phone-tree coordinator—the person responsible for notifying other team members when support is required. Appoint a backup phone-tree coordinator in case she is the member needing support.

✧ Suggest each member become familiar with *Share the Care: How to Organize a Group to Care for Someone Who is Seriously Ill*. See p. 231. This book will help you flesh out the roles your team may need to assume. It also describes the importance of having a leader and coordinator for your team so that the many tasks can be delegated and their accomplishment assured.

✧ Create a list of ideas to pursue at future meetings. These might include: exploring the available medical and support resources in your community; preparing and discussing end-of-life documents in a group setting (see p. 181); practicing ways to initiate conversations regarding end-of-life issues with your family members (see p. 166); or discussing the resistance and denial of such conversations in our society.

Knowing that help is available with a single phone call to the phone-tree coordinator will be one step that is already in place.

A RESOURCE CENTER FOR CARING

Imagine a nearby place where you could visit and find:

✧ Books and pamphlets related to specific diseases and treatments

✧ Names of local caregiving agencies and organizations

✧ A roster of local nurses, social workers, and other caregivers that are available for giving temporary, part-time or full-time care, or guidance

✧ The opportunity to become part of that roster if you are a nurse or social worker that would like to work only in your own community

✧ Ongoing support groups for caregivers, bereavement, and education

✧ Names of other people who have gone through similar situations that are willing to share the knowledge they gained

✧ A system of matching up those who need live-in companionship and aid with those who need a place to live and have talents to give

Does your community have such a place? If not, would you be interested in helping create one? The basis for a resource center may already be in place in an existing senior or community center. Such an establishment could serve as a clearinghouse during a personal illness but also when a natural or political disaster occurs. It could also be an important extension of your personal team.

To learn how one particular community provided many of these resources, visit the Beach Cities Health District. See p. 239.

EXERCISE

PREPARE YOUR END-OF-LIFE DOCUMENTS IN A GROUP SETTING

Most of us think it is a good idea to write down our wishes in wills, trusts, advance directives, and power of attorney. However, many do not follow through.

If we have created such documents, they are often not honored because their contents have not been discussed with those involved. Family members may not know where the documents are kept. Also, the documents need to be updated at least every two years, or more often as changes occur.

Consider inviting your team over for a potluck lunch or dinner for the purpose of preparing end-of-life documents. Not only will this accomplish the overdue task, it can be fun and enriching to share feelings and discuss the potential responses to the required questions.

Preparation can include rereading Part II (chapters 4–12) of this book. Ask your guests to bring questions they have, notebooks to record ideas, and actual forms to fill out. The Durable Power of Attorney for Health Care and Five Wishes can be downloaded from the Internet. See p. 222.

Discussing what quality of life means to each member present will initiate stimulating conversation and help make decisions that will be written in the documents. For example, under what conditions would you want your life extended? What kinds of treatments are you willing to live with? What kind of help are you willing to have if you become ill? Have other members experienced situations from which they learned new information or at least learned that they didn't know enough? What are the pros and cons of burial and cremation? Are there great differences in costs between the two and among the businesses that provide these services? Whom do you trust to be your proxy if you can't speak for yourself? Would a friend be better in that role than a family member?

After these conversations are held, a second meeting could take place in which the documents are completed and witnessed. Information about where they will be located and who will be given copies can also be shared.

FACING THE MYSTERIES IN PERSON

After reading her copy of Facing the Final Mystery, *a friend's daughter asked her family to meet when she and her sister were both in town for the holidays. She was moved to have this gathering after discussing the issue of cremation and burial with her husband. They had never talked about this during their twenty years together and she learned they had opposite points of view. She began wondering what would have taken place had they not discussed it.*

Each family member had filled out the "Five Wishes" forms before meeting. They sat in a circle and started with the topic of choosing a proxy. Each person said who they chose as proxy and why. Gwen's logical choice was her husband. However, since filling out her form, he had suffered injuries in a car-accident and she realized he would not be able to carry out the duties of proxy for some time. Gwen decided she would ask her sister to be a co-proxy for health care. Ruth had selected her boyfriend, since she was temporarily away at school. While considering her choice of him as proxy, she began to have questions about other facets of their relationship.

Over two hours had passed by the time they got to the fifth wish. They were hungry, and more noteworthy, were hysterically laughing, making up possible scenarios of celebrations and body-part donations. The family learned a lot about each other, had fun, and decided to meet again and share any changes, as well as additional thoughts that were likely to arise.

On a separate occasion, a group of seven of my friends gathered, each one asking for the meeting because they could not seem to complete their advance directives.

Samuel had asked his twin brother Moses to be his proxy. Moses said he had no interest in discussing "that stuff," and Samuel didn't know what to do next since he believed only a family member should fill this roll. We discussed the possibilities of close friends whom he could ask.

On the other hand, Barbara had chosen her two best friends because they were both nurses and understood her philosophy of life and death. The problem was that they lived 8,000 miles from California. Again, we encouraged Barbara to consider some of her nurse-friends who lived nearby, as possible proxies.

Helen's issue was that she wanted her husband and son, as first and second proxies, to support her unusual wishes of being "made comfortable" if she collapsed on to the floor without calling 911. Neither relative was willing to agree to this request. The group helped her decide it would be a good idea to have a family meeting where Helen could feel supported. Then she could explain why she didn't want to be taken to a hospital.

This meeting also ended with lots of laughter and imaginative solutions to end-of-life problems. It seemed to me that once the topic was put on the table, it was not morbid; in fact it brought forth both humor and creativity as well as completion of the documents.

ACTION STEPS

1.   *Create* a team. Have an informal potluck gathering and present the ideas in this chapter. See what kind of interest or feedback takes place. Decide what steps to take next, such as inviting more people or asking for help in setting up a second meeting.

2. Suggest that your *book group* select and discuss any of the books from the CAREGIVING Section (p. 231) of the annotated bibliography.

3. *Spiritual or religious centers* are traditionally a main source of providing help in times of crisis. Learn how your place of worship provides care, who to contact if you need help, and how you can participate in giving help in times of crisis.

4. *Service organizations,* such as the Optimists or Elks, exist to help people or causes. Find out how your service group helps their own members if illness or death occurs. If your chapter has different topics at monthly meetings, talk to the program chairperson and ask that the issues of caregiving, team building, and service within the organization be discussed.

5. *Your neighborhood* may contain the people who are most likely to be present when a crisis occurs, especially if it takes place while you are at home. Talk with your neighbors about the idea of supporting each other in difficult times. Learn who are more likely to need help because they live alone. Exchange phone numbers and names of doctors and relatives that may need to be called in an emergency.

6. Learn about existing health resource groups outside the medical establishment, which provide information and support such as Wellness Community and Our House. See p. 255 and p. 238.

Energy gathers
Hands reach to touch each other
Love lights up the room

EG

Seventeen

Advocate For Yourself, Your Family and Friends, Your Patients and Clients, and Your Community

What you do, what you say, what you are, may help others in ways
you never know. Your influence, like your shadow,
extends where you may never be.

—— Anonymous

REDUCING ERROR; IMPROVING CARE

To advocate is to plead or take action for the cause of another. Advocates are either an *individual* who "pleads" or *more than one person* who is part of a team or an advocacy group. In earlier chapters, we discussed the benefits of conversations about end-of-life issues; early use of hospice; the relationship of quality of life to medical choices; the importance and misuse of advance directives; and the challenges of caregiving. Now it is time to make sure these concepts are used and supported.

While advocacy may appear as a challenge to authority, its plead invites extra clarity and caution concerning the *what, why,* and *how long* regarding medical, financial, practical and spiritual end-of-life issues.

What is an advocate?

Being an advocate can be as simple as asking pertinent questions to your mother's doctor, and as complicated as creating a political amendment that will change the way health care is administered. Advocacy may include managing the resources of a sick family member, or opening the door to the potential richness of the dying experience to those who are afraid or repulsed by it.

Why do we need advocacy?

Our medical care system has changed rapidly in the last fifty years, without the education and support necessary to insure good patient care within those changes. Where once a family had a single doctor, one community hospital, and no life extending "tubes," we now have specialists, more than one doctor prescribing medications, and machines and treatments with names we can't pronounce. Who will coordinate the recommended treatments, make sure the patient's wishes are heard, and see that communication remains open in all directions?

Large corporations now run for-profit hospitals with the main goal being cost control rather than excellent patient care. Who will see that you or a loved one is cared for in a hospital when one registered nurse must oversee scores of patients; the nurses' aides, while kind and of good intent, often speak little English; and many doctors are untrained in speaking the truth to a dying patient?

New drugs are approved in short periods of time, often without adequate knowledge of side effects and long-term use results. Who will read the fine print on your parent's prescription, as well as checking for the possible contraindications of using several drugs at one time?

Who is an advocate?

Qualifications for being an advocate: your willingness and ability to gather information, your desire to share your findings with families, friends, and the medical team, and time to devote to the specific needs of the moment.

Anyone may become an advocate-in-training. When a loved one is ill, all family members and even neighbors and friends can become advocates for her best interests. Every time she enters the medical system, situations will arise that offer an opportunity to advocate for more effective care.

If you don't know where to turn, there are professional advocates. The most important one is called a case worker or care manager. A care manager may be a social worker, counselor, or nurse. They may help with transitions, oversee quality of medical treatment, access needed services, and direct patients and their families to resources within the community.

You will likely become an advocate at some point in time, first for yourself, then for your loved ones, patients and clients, and, finally, for your community or larger society. A little information and preparation makes this role easier to assume.

ADVOCATING FOR YOURSELF

Advocacy begins with caring for yourself. You cannot effectively provide long-term care for someone else if you haven't attended to your needs first. You can be your own best advocate by taking any or all of the following steps:

    ★   Examine your fear. Have your fears of dying, death, or illness kept you from having regular medical checkups?

    ★   Get health insurance if you don't already have it.

    ★   Ask a friend to be your advocate if you are hospitalized.

    ★   Create your team for future health care needs. Using the information in chapter 15 and the book *Share the Care,* initiate a meeting in which such ideas are discussed. Focus on the idea that all participants will be able to receive care, in turn, from the team members.

MARTHA'S FEAR

Martha had several relatives with breast cancer. She was so afraid of getting it herself that she postponed, visits to a doctor for years. She also did not do self-examinations on her breasts. By the time a lump became large enough to see, cancer had spread to her lungs.

ADVOCATING FOR YOUR FRIENDS AND FAMILY

Advocacy becomes part of the circle of mutual caregiving that grows out of a healthy community. Not only do we benefit from being an advocate for ourselves, it also sets the stage for participating in a community of care.

★ Volunteer to be an advocate for a friend who is hospitalized. Ira Byock, MD, suggests staying in the hospital with a very ill person to make sure he gets needed and prescribed care, and to prevent unwanted or possibly unnecessary interventions. Even if your friend has created advance directives and informed his personal doctor of his wishes, he may be left alone and vulnerable to other medical caregivers who change shifts and may not always pass on the pertinent information.

★ Accompany loved ones to their doctor appointments and take notes. If your family member is elderly, she may not remember important instructions from the doctor.

★ Keep a current list of your loved one's medications, including herbs and vitamins, and their daily dosage. This list should be taken to every doctor visit and updated as needed. If more than one doctor is involved, the list is especially important. If you feel comfortable with medical terminology, another level of advocacy includes checking for contraindications and side effects of medications.

★ For home care, check the professional caregiver's credentials and resumé. Do a background check. Keep a watchful eye on daily care, if you have a loved one who is ill and living at home. Watch that medications are not being stolen or abused by the caregiver.

★ Participate in creating a team for your family member who needs care.

EUGENIA: "HOW WILL I GET TO THE DOCTOR IF YOU DON'T TAKE ME?"

Eugenia had been comfortably and easily placed in an attractive senior residence. The extended family was relieved

*that she was happy with her new surroundings, played
Bingo nightly, and was relieved to not cook her own meals.*

*No one noticed that her daughter, Alison, was stressed
to the point of exhaustion. She was the only family member
to take care of Eugenia's needs outside the residence:
shopping for personal items; driving her to doctor's
appointments, physical therapy treatments, and occasional
lunches out. It had never occurred to her to ask for help—
not unlike many first-born daughters—even though there
were grown grandchildren and capable in-laws in the
neighborhood.*

*When Alison's brother, Sam, visited from out of town,
he recognized Alison's stress. By the time he left a week
later, he had enlisted other family members who were
pleased to assume specific roles for meeting Eugenia's needs.
A month later Alison reported how relieved she felt by the
support, and how excited she was to sign up for an art class
since she now had free time. The other family members are
happy to be spending more time with Eugenia.*

ADVOCATING FOR BETTER END-OF-LIFE CARE
IN YOUR COMMUNITY

Public outcry and demand has historically been a primary means in
which social change takes place. Increased life expectancy and long-
term chronic illnesses have pushed improved end-of-life care near
the top of important social advocacy issues. Now when a family
member or friend needs our attention, we become active
participants in this historic social change.

The simple steps include:
- ★   Increasing the comfort with which we discuss dying and
  death
- ★   Encouraging the use of advance directives
- ★   Planning for end-of-life care *before* a medical crisis occurs

★ Spreading knowledge and benefits of hospice and palliative care

The larger steps can be:

★ Helping to reform health care insurance availability and costs of medical care

★ Seeking improved nursing home care

★ Creating and promoting new ways of caring and housing for our elderly

★ Getting involved with health care reform political advocacy

HOSPICE CARE CAME TOO LATE
FOR LILLY

Lilly's initial diagnosis was advanced bone cancer and her prognosis was poor—six months at the most. Because she and her husband intended to "beat" the cancer, they pursued alternative treatments once the medical recommendations were exhausted. These treatments did extend her life to sixteen months. However, the comfort care that she needed during that time, such as a motorized wheelchair and oxygen, were procured by her husband, Raymond, after hours of research and using all of their available funds. Hospice care was available to Lilly from the start because of her "terminal" diagnosis, and would have provided all of the above and more, leaving Raymond to spend more time with Lilly. Their doctor didn't suggest hospice and they did not know to ask for it.

It wasn't until the final days of her life that a friend stopped by and determined that Lilly needed better pain management and that hospice should be called.

The following examples illustrate how two communities became advocates for end-of-life care.

COMMUNITY AGREEMENT
IN USING ADVANCE DIRECTIVES

In Sonoma County, California, residents and paramedics agreed together that a specifically colored—goldenrod—advance directive, expressing the medical desires of the resident, could be found attached to the refrigerator door. In Contra Costa County, California, the community decided upon a covered butter dish inside the refrigerator to hold their documents. Through community meetings, the location of these documents was made known to all that might be involved, should illness or emergencies occur.

Dr. Ira Byock suggests that until this is accomplished in your community, do not call an ambulance if your loved one does not want to be resuscitated. Emergency medical technicians and ER staff are trained and required by law to resuscitate unless a DNR states otherwise.

In each of the categories described in this chapter—self, family and community—you can take action and create change. If in your estimation, you know someone who has suffered a grave medical injustice related to end-of-life treatments, congratulations! You are part of a large (and growing) crisis in medicine. If you want to prevent this injustice from occurring to you or your loved ones, you can become part of the solution by being an advocate.

ACTION STEPS

1. Join AARP (formerly called the American Association for Retired Persons). For only $12.50 per year—reduced fee for second spouse—anyone age fifty and older is can join. AARP has become one of the largest advocacy groups in America for rights and laws related to the needs of seniors. See p. 223.

2. Contact your political representatives so they can help you champion end-of-life causes, describing personal experiences that have caused unneeded pain and upheaval related to you or your family. If you can offer solutions, change can ultimately be initiated with the help of amendments added to your state's constitution. See p. 224 for easy ways to make these contacts.

3. Locate existing organizations that champion causes important to you personally, such as the Alzheimer's or Arthritis foundations. Access these organizations by typing the name or category of the illness into your Internet search engine. Find out how you can become part of their advocacy team.

4. Watch "On Our Own Terms: Moyers on Dying in America" especially if you missed its initial airing in September of 2000. See p. 235.

5. Contact your clergy person and encourage discussion of end-of-life issues to take place within the organization's smaller groups, as well as in the weekly sermon or message.

6. Select any of the books from the annotated bibliography to be read by your book-group, followed by discussion and creation of steps to take.

7. Suggest topics for monthly meetings in your clubs and organizations. They can become forums for all the issues in

this book. Encourage the program chairperson to set up a series of topics on end-of-life issues. Contact authors of the books listed in the bibliography to speak at your monthly meetings.

8.   Write letters to the editor, which address end-of-life issues. Magazine and newspaper articles can become a stimulus for your involvement, and keep the topic in the public eye. Also, you may write letters drawing attention to events or speakers in your community regarding end-of-life issues.

9.   Follow up any medical infractions you have encountered by making phone calls or writing letters to persons or institutions where the event occurred, as well as to local newspapers, so the public can participate in helping to prevent recurrences.

10.   Express support regarding medical situations that were handled well to encourage continuing good care.

11.   Learn more about organizations that advocate for end-of-life issues. See p. 222.

$\star$
$\star$ $\star$

*S*peaking from the heart

Feelings are flowing freely

A new world opens

C.W.

Eighteen

Visualize Your Dreams

If you don't have a dream, your life will be about your problems.
—— Joyce Chapman, MA, *Live Your Dream: Discover and Achieve Your Life Purpose*

WHAT IS THE STUFF THAT DREAMS ARE MADE OF?

This is the last chapter. By now, you have taken care of the business of living and dying; cleaned up relationships that have gone astray; and written at least one letter to an editor or government official to promote change in end-of-life care. Right? Good job!

But what about you? You and your glorious, days, weeks, years or decades. What does your heart desire? Are your innate talents and gifts lying dormant? Has your true purpose been expressed? Do you even know what your purpose is? The following stories show the diverse sources from which inspiration is born.

A DISCOVERY OF MEANING

Victor Frankl spent several years in German concentration camps and lost his entire family. During that time, he struggled to find meaning in the horrific experiences they were all enduring. He watched young and healthy people succumb while older and more infirm people continued living, and he wondered why. He learned that the one choice we all have is our attitude (and its exercise through of our own will) to determine how we face our circumstances. He describes this time and his resulting philosophy (logotherapy) in his book, *Man's Search for Meaning*. Without meaning, we can only continue living if we fill our days with distractions. Facing and embracing the final mystery—that we will suffer and we will die—leads us to the real meaning of our life.

Now is the time to envision our future so that when death does arrive, at its mysterious, chosen moment, we can acknowledge that we have spent our days wisely and kindly, manifested our destinies, and shared our gifts with others.

JAPANESE TEA CEREMONY

The Japanese tea ceremony illustrates in a symbolic way, the fleeting passage of life, especially in the flower-arranging portion. The tea-master gathers flowers and chooses a specific vase. She arranges them during the ceremony. Only wild flowers or delicate, short-lived fruit blossoms are used to remind the guests that life is short, like the plum petals, and we must make the most of it.

TYING ROCKS TO CLOUDS

William Elliott was twelve the year both of his parents died. His loss, grief, and anger propelled him to search for the meaning of life. "How can people live in a world with death and not ask about death and about life?" he asked. At first he asked anyone who would listen to his questions. Then he decided the famous spiritual leaders of the world would have the answers. He made a list of questions and a list of important people, and borrowed a typewriter. The letter requesting interviews was copied with the name of the recipient typed in later. "It looked terrible. It looked like one of those chain letters you get in the mail with your name pitifully typed at the top," described Elliot.

His friends did not encourage him. They said no one would answer the letter. And furthermore, they reminded William that he had no credentials. And that he lived in a trailer. Many people did not respond. Many others responded and said it was a nice project but they didn't have time.

However, many on his list did agree to be interviewed, including Elisabeth Kübler-Ross, Norman Vincent Peale, Ram Dass, Rabbi Harold Kushner, the Dalai Lama, Mother Teresa, Pir Vilayat Khan, and more. Their responses and Elliott's description of his travels to visit each of them comprise one of the most delightful books I've ever read, *Tying Rocks to Clouds: Meetings and Conversations with Wise and Spiritual People.*

Some of the questions he posed were: "On what main beliefs or truths do you base your life? Do you believe in God? What is the purpose in life? What is the highest ideal that a person can reach? What is the greatest obstacle to that ideal?"

But more important than the content is the ability to witness a "regular" person, like you or me, create his dream and then follow it into completion in this very readable and inspiring book. It took six years to collect the interviews. Lack of money, credentials, fame, or geography did not stop him.

What is your dream? Who inspires you? Where will your next step lead you?

WHERE DO YOU GO FROM UP?

Former President Jimmy Carter admits to being devastated from leaving the White House after only one term in office. A very difficult time followed—personally, financially, and in his relationship with his wife Rosalynn. Things looked grim, he says, until "We finally had the courage to do what everybody needs to do: to sit down in a time of quiet contemplation and say, 'OK, what is there that I have? What are my talents? What are my abilities?'"

He has since founded and led the Carter Center in Atlanta, which mediates difficult political and health related situations around the world; written fourteen books; and volunteered with Habitat for Humanity. The Carters feel that their years since the White House have been the most rewarding of their lives. In his most recent book, *The Virtues of Aging*, Carter also describes how fulfilling his dreams and expressing his talents have contributed to facing death with equanimity. He and Rosalynn prepared living wills that preclude artificial measures to sustain life...pointing out that a large portion of Medicare payments go to the last year of a person's life.

EXCEPTIONALLY INTERESTING AND CREATIVE ORDINARY PEOPLE

Carol Adrienne tells the story of how the combination of people, events, illness, knowledge, and background led her to find her true purpose. She explored the lives of many people who wondered and moved into, floundered and found, suffered and achieved new ways of expressing their abilities. She shares these stories, along with principles and techniques for creating change, in her book, *The Purpose of Your Life: Finding Your Place in the World Using Synchronicity, Intuition, and Uncommon Sense*. The book is peppered with inspiring quotes, useful exercises, and many examples of how purpose is discovered and put to good use.

Following are exercises and action steps to help you crystallize your talents, visions, and purpose, so that when you look back you are pleased with the legacy that is left to your immediate survivors, your communities, and your world.

EXERCISES

WRITING YOUR OWN EULOGY

A eulogy is described as "a spoken or written composition in praise of a person's life or character." In writing your own eulogy, you have the opportunity to examine what you hope someone who cares for you *will* say after you have died. You may also be moved to put into action now some of the qualities or accomplishments you *want* to have happen.

This is an exercise that invites you to create the most positive, exciting, memorable "you." Let your imaginative powers soar, and describe everything you hope will be remembered about you. Be expansive, colorful, and don't forget humor. This may be the truth for you now, or it may present itself to you as goals to be met. Have fun!

When you are finished, share it with a friend or two. Have one of them read it back to you. Ask them to join you in the exercise and read theirs to you. Discuss together the parts that you are proud of already, and the parts that you added on for future consideration.

If there are ideas, dreams, or goals you haven't achieved yet, put them on a "to do" or a "to be" list. Ask your friends to witness your commitment to accomplish some cherished desires. Pay attention to how you feel as you listen to your accomplishments during this life.

This exercise can also be done from the "critic's" point of view, instead of from a place of praise. It is unfortunately much easier for most people to list their faults and failings. If you want to continue to explore this technique, try this "critic's eulogy" as a way of examining what qualities you are unhappy with, or what feats you have not yet accomplished. Add a "to change" category to your "to do" and "to be" lists.

FOCUS GROUP

Invite two or three friends to meet with you on a weekly basis for the purpose of keeping each other "on track." Discuss how such a meeting could benefit each member in the best way and create a mission statement that might include how often you meet, the method in which you share your goals and accomplishments, and the amount of time you devote to this project.

I have met with Diane and Kriss each Friday at a coffee shop for several years. After munching pastries and catching up on the week's inner and outer events, we use a council format (see p. 169) to present the steps we have taken towards our current goals or projects. These topics change over time and have included work-related tasks (such as how to increase the number of clients or implementing new kinds of workshops), to larger work-related decisions (such as making complete career changes).

The focus group has allowed me to observe and accomplish all the tasks involved in writing this book, from researching, writing, editing, promoting, answering publishing questions, and overcoming frustration.

At the end of each meeting, we announce what we hope to accomplish by the following Friday, bringing clarity to a portion of what lies ahead and decreasing the overwhelming feelings when the project seems enormous. We all agree that on Thursday evening, when we examine our stated commitments, we feel glad that something "out there" is nudging us to completion. Sometimes this results in staying up very late to finish what we had planned. On other occasions, we feel gleeful that the job is done. Sometimes we have done even more and look forward to sharing the news.

ACTION STEPS

1. Make a list of "adult roles" you imagined for yourself when you were a child (fireman, detective, auto mechanic, dancer, or forest ranger). Are there any that still hold power for you? Any that you can still find a way to make come true? Are there roles you are ready and willing to relinquish?

2. Are there talents or gifts you know you have but never thought were good enough to develop, like piano, watercolor, or the tango? Is it possible for you to develop them now? Try listing them and pursue at least one.

3. Are there skills you have always wanted to develop such as gardening, woodworking, or a new language? Make a list of them and choose one to pursue.

4. Are there political, environmental, or social causes that make your pulse race with either anger or joy? Have you put any of your energy into those arenas with time, money, or ideas? Can you see any ways to do that now? Which ideologies or organizations would you like to support now?

5. Is there a way you can incorporate more rest, relaxation, and introspection? More naps? More novels to read? When will you schedule your next massage?

6. Are there people you would like to meet? Get to know better? Make a list of them and the steps you need to find them.

7. Is there a spiritual path you have wanted to explore? Take the first step in learning more about a noted teacher, preacher, or healer.

Blooming flowers please
Tree bird's song waves carry joy
Renewal of life, it's Spring

B.D.

Epilogue

*Death is no enemy but the
foundation of gratitude, sympathy and art.
Of all life's pleasures, only love owes no debt to death.*

— Anita Diamant, *The Red Tent*

My parents have quietly guided me through this project. They don't know that. My mother's fear of the dying process—and her very verbal expression of that fear—led me to the library and Amazon.com for books. The stories I read, as well as those told by friends and colleagues, fueled this book. They also helped me help my parents die. That is, I was able to let my parents die "naturally" when their times came.

When my mother survived a mild heart attack, just before her 87th birthday, she got a gleam in her eye. Maybe her body would let her escape after all. She "hurt all over" she would say; she couldn't sleep; she itched; food didn't taste good and she was tired. Polio as a child had possibly contributed to severe muscle and joint pain. While she could still swim, she could no longer walk across the sand to get into her beloved ocean, and getting out of a pool became impossible. She couldn't drive any more and my father's dementia was driving her nuts! While his repeated sentences amused me, they made her scream at him. That made him drink more wine. That made her scream at him more. It was not a pretty picture.

Yet, her organic systems functioned better than mine. She could eat raw onions and garlic. Her blood pressure was normal. No diabetes. No kidney problems. No previously known heart problems.

After my mother's heart attack, the attending physician, a kind young woman, prescribed two medications. I asked the purpose of the pills. The doctor said, in front of my mother, "to keep her alive longer."

A few weeks later, my mom reported "These damn pills are making me woozy and nauseated." She quit taking them and became the happiest I'd seen her in a decade. She stopped complaining about everything, including my father, who by this time was living in a nursing home. She even stopped grumbling about my ex-husband. She and I had great conversations, saw some good movies, and enjoyed playing gin rummy together.

The Tuesday before she died, I picked up both of my parents to take them to lunch. I had begun visiting them separately because of their bickering, but with her new attitude adjustment, I could see her revived love for my dad. We went to her favorite restaurant—the Sizzler—where she exclaimed how delicious everything tasted. I started to get a feeling that something big was happening. Two days later, she reported a "funny breathing thing." I asked if she wanted me to take her to the doctor. "No," she said, "I'll take a little walk." She called back later to say she felt fine.

The next day I called her at noon and there was no answer. I had a feeling that she might have had another heart attack, but I knew how strongly she felt about not lingering and about not having "tubes." Because I was comfortable with death and with her leaving when her body stopped functioning, I did not call her building or 911. A few hours later, I received a call and learned that my mother's neighbor became concerned after not seeing my mom since breakfast. Upon entering my mother's apartment, she found her lying on the floor, not breathing.

Despite the shock and loss one feels when a parent dies, I was grateful that she was able to go quickly and avoid the slow, painful, dying process that she had feared for so long. During many of our discussions, I had encouraged my mother to replace her mournful image of dying with the possibility of a peaceful death. I like to believe that this helped her. She had prepared well. I had assured her I would look after my father if she died before him. Her papers were in order, her drawers and closets pared down, and an advertisement taped to her refrigerator said, "I'm ready!" She had added, "For Whatever!"

My father's journey to the other side was quite different. To my surprise, he lived another three-and-a-half years after my mother died. I thought their sixty years of marriage would draw him to her soon after she left. I guess that he had more work to do.

During my weekly visits with him, and our saunter to a nearby café, he recalled the people and experiences of his past. Many of these recollections were of the time he spent in Denmark as a boy, even though those years comprised less than a quarter of his long life. He verbally painted pictures of riding his bicycle through the forest to the next town where he had apprenticed as an auto mechanic. He loved teaching people to drive, often in their first car, and enjoyed being invited to his student's homes for coffee, cakes, and an occasional beer.

Sometimes he recalled events of my childhood, driving me and my friends to the ice skating rink in Pasadena, taking us to the snow at Mt. Wilson, and our family vacations to Yosemite and Newport Beach. Often, he would ask me about particular old friends, and was always shocked when I told him they had died, sometimes twenty years earlier. He also could not believe he had lived into his 90s. When I asked how old he thought he was, he usually guessed that he was 67 or 72 years old.

Eight months before he died, he fell and broke his arm. His

arm healed remarkably well, but the incident initiated the deterioration of the rest of his body. His strength gradually disappeared so that he could not walk. Sitting in a wheelchair the last few months became difficult and he yearned to get back into bed after being up a short time. He seemed to be pain free and I am sure that this physical ease allowed him to retain his lovely manners until the end. Four months before he died, I initiated hospice care, knowing they could become my support team and my dad's ticket to comfort. I will be forever grateful that I knew to ask, and that they were at our sides during those weeks of gradual slowing down.

On a Monday, my father turned a corner. I could see his expression was somewhat blank, although when I began crying at this loss, he also shed tears. By the afternoon, he slipped into a deep sleep. On Wednesday, he seemed to rouse a bit, opened his eyes and smiled a couple of times when spoken to, and then slipped back into the deep sleep. I sat with him for five days. As the hospice team visited, we conferred about the meaning of each sign or symptom. My younger son spent two afternoons at grandpa's side, stroking his arm and expressing his appreciation of my dad. By Friday, I could see that my dad's breathing was becoming more shallow and quiet. I sensed the end was near. That night I curled up in his old green recliner and dozed, checking on him every hour or so. At four in the morning he was breathing. At five he was not.

My husband arrived and together we bathed and dressed my father in his old suit, now many sizes too big for him. The effect was touching and even somewhat amusing. There was a lightness in the room, as if something great had been accomplished. We lit candles and placed photographs of my parents on the nightstand. The caregivers of the nursing home came in to touch him and offer their condolences.

My mother and my father had allowed me to see that death could be peaceful and pain free. With my father, I was able to watch his soft tissues shrink after he lost his desire to eat and drink, and I learned that I wasn't horrified to watch him become emaciated. I was able to witness that "not hydrating" him allowed his death to be easier. He had no rattling cough; the decrease of bodily fluids kept him drier and, therefore, needing to be moved less often. I felt the quiet naturalness of dying and death. My mother's sudden departure, while initially shocking, matched her style of making quick decisions and her impatience in general. The saying that "one dies as one lives" was certainly illustrated to me by both my mother's and father's passages.

My parents had also initiated me into the comfort of discussing end-of-life issues. They had made wills and filled out advance directives years earlier, as well as prepaying for their cremations. The three of us talked freely about their wishes. My mother and I had put my name jointly on their remaining bank accounts, so I was able to pay my father's rent with his social security money. There were no financial concerns or surprises.

I am grateful for their teachings. I am grateful for their peaceful deaths.

PART IV

Resources

Continuing the journey after reading the book.

Appendix I

Glossary

Glossary Note: If you cannot find a term in the GLOSSARY, refer to INDEX. The first reference in the text may include a brief description.

advance directives: Legally binding documents (including **DNR**, **DPA for H**, **Five Wishes**, **Living Will**) that allow one to put in writing, desired end-of-life health care choices as well as designating a proxy to oversee those choices.

> **DNR (do not resuscitate):** States only the wish to not be revived after the heart or breath has stopped.

> **DPA for H (durable power of attorney for health care):** A formal document in which desired end-of-life medical wishes are written and a proxy is designated. May also be called a medical power of attorney or health care power of attorney. Legal state by state.

> **Five Wishes:** A more user friendly and expanded version of the **DPA for H.** Legally accepted in forty states.

> **Living Will:** An earlier version of the **DPA for H** that includes only desired medical wishes and not the selection of a proxy. Living Will is sometimes used generically as a term for **advance directives**.

> **naked DPA of H:** Gives the proxy complete discretion to decide on types of treatment, if the patient is unable to communicate.

> **proxy for health care:** The person(s) who are designated to make health care decisions for someone that cannot communicate on his own behalf. May also be called a health care proxy or agent for health care.

advocate: A person or group who defends, maintains, or pleads a cause (or proposal) for one's own or another's sake.

agent for financial power of attorney: The person(s) you designate to make financial and legal decisions in the event you become incapacitated and cannot sign checks or conduct business.

anticipatory grief: Grief that is experienced from an impending loss or death.

assisted suicide: See **euthanasia**.

autopsy: Surgical examination after death to determine cause of death.

bereavement: The emotional or psychological state after suffering a great loss.

bioethics: The ethical consideration of medical practice, health care delivery, and biological research.

bioethical dilemma: A situation regarding bioethical issues, that occurs due to lack of knowledge or failure to communicate.

cardiac arrest: Sudden cessation of the heart beat.

care manager (case worker): One who is assigned to or hired by a patient for the purpose of attaining necessary treatment, equipment, supplies, and organizational and financial assistance. Often a social worker.

cardiopulmonary resuscitation (CPR): The re-stimulation of the heart beat and breath after a cardiac arrest or respiratory failure.

case worker: See **care-manager**.

code-blue: In a hospital setting, the sound that alerts and requests the resuscitation team to rush to the scene of a **cardiac arrest** or **respiratory failure**.

comfort care (palliative care): Provides pain management and relief of other distressing symptoms without necessarily seeking a cure.

council: A method of communication in which participants focus only on the person who is speaking, awaiting their own turn to respond or speak. There is no "cross-talk" (interruption) while the person speaks.

CPR: See **cardiopulmonary resuscitation**.

deathbed visions: What both the dying and the caregivers have heard, seen, smelled and felt, at or near death.

death with dignity (right to die): A movement that seeks having a choice about the way in which they die, especially the legal right to physician-assisted suicide.

diagnosis: Determination of a disease which is producing symptoms in a patient.

dialysis: The exchange of molecules through a semi-permeable membrane. Utilized in renal (kidney) dialysis for the purpose of cleansing the blood of toxins.

DNR: See **advance directives**.

Do Not Resuscitate (DNR): See **advance directives**.

DPA for H: See **advance directives**.

Durable Power of Attorney for Healthcare: See **advance directives**.

embalming: The practice of injecting a formaldehyde-based fluid into the arterial system of a dead body for the purpose of disinfecting and preserving the body.

epitaph: An inscription on a tomb or gravestone in memory of the one buried there.

estate planning: Counsel to determine the best ways to allocate money and other assets; often includes **advance directives**.

eulogy: Literally, "good words" about a person who has died. Often spoken at a funeral or memorial service.

euthanasia (**assisted suicide**:) When one person helps another to die, including:

> **active euthansia**: Helping the patient die by administering drugs or treatment, e.g. giving a high dose of a narcotic.
>
> **involuntary euthanasia** (**mercy killing**): When a person helps a patient to die without the request or consent of the patient.
>
> **passive euthanasia**: Helping the patient die by withholding treatment, e.g. withholding antibiotics during extreme infection.
>
> **physician-assisted suicide**: When the patient requests the help of a physician to die. The legalization of physician's participation is a major goal of the right to die or death with dignity movements.
>
> **voluntary euthanasia**: Assisted suicide at the request and with the consent of the patient.

executor: The person designated to carry out the terms written in a will.

financial power of attorney: A document that allows you to name an agent to conduct specified financial and legal business for you when you are unable to do so.

Five Wishes: See **advance directives**.

Funeral Rule: Created by the Federal Trade Commission to prohibit funeral providers from making untrue claims about products or services.

grief: The inner or personal response to losing someone or something we love.

health care power of attorney: See **durable power of attorney for health care**.

health care proxy: See **proxy for health care under advance directives**.

hospice: A philosophy or program of care rather than a place; a blend of services that addresses the physical, emotional, and spiritual needs of the family and terminally ill patient.

involuntary euthanasia: See **euthanasia**.

joint-titles: Creates the opportunity for more than one person to sign on a checking account and other financial documents, allowing for smooth transition at the time of death.

living will: See **advance directives**.

long-term care insurance (LTC): Created specifically for those needing long-term care in a nursing home, taking up the slack that is not covered by Medicare and health insurance.

LTC: See **long-term care insurance**.

Medicaid: A federal government program designed to provide aid for those unable to afford health care insurance.

medical power of attorney: See **durable power of attorney for health care**.

mercy killing (involuntary euthansia): See **euthansia**.

mourning: The outer expression of grief; the external actions taken to cope with loss.

naked Durable Power of Attorney for Health: See **advance directives**.

NDE: See **near-death experience**.

near-death experience (NDE): A collection of common qualities (such as bright light, a long tunnel, familiar faces) experienced by people who come close to death—or possibly die and are revived—often leading to life-transformations.

no-code: In a hospital setting, it means that the patient does not want a code-blue response following cardiac arrest or respiratory failure.

obituary: Notice of a person's death, often appearing in a newspaper, containing biographical information, cause of death and names of surviving relatives.

palliate: To abate or reduce symptoms.

palliative care: See **comfort care**.

passive euthansia: See **euthanasia**.

pay-on-death: A financial arrangement in which the titles of documents (e.g. deeds and stocks) and bank accounts can transfer directly at the time of death to a designated agent.

persistent vegetative state: Brain (cerebral) death, due to overwhelming damage of the brain from severe head injury or lack of oxygen. The autonomic and motor reflexes continue to function despite the brain death.

physician-assisted suicide: See **euthanasia**.

power of attorney: See **financial power of attorney**.

probate: The legal process in which a judge authenticates a will and changes the titles of property and bank accounts to the heirs.

prognosis: The probable course and outcome of a medical condition including the estimated chance of recovery.

proxy for health care: See **advance directives**.

respite care: Help given to caregivers, during a period of (usually long-term) caregiving.

resuscitation: Restoration to life after apparent death, including restarting the heart and breath.

right to die: See **death with dignity**.

role-playing: A tool to practice conversations in which one assumes the role of a particular family member. It fosters understanding of another's point of view and learning new ways to communicate.

shadow: A psychological term that refers to some part of our ego or personality that is hidden from us.

shock: Medically, depression of body function, usually associated with lowered blood volume, following physical, emotional, or mental excitement or trauma.

suicide: Taking one's own life, usually as a result of depression that has not been treated or relieved by treatment.

thanatologist: One who studies, teaches, and counsels about the issues related to dying and death.

thanatology: The study of dying and death.

trust: A financial document that states who controls our assets while we are alive and what will happen to them when we die.

ventilator: A mechanical device causing airflow into the lungs of a person who cannot breath on his own.

voluntary euthanasia: See **euthanasia**.

wake: A gathering of friends and family around the deceased, prior to burial, sometimes accompanied by festivity.

will: A legal document that allows: naming of an executor; selection of a guardian for dependents; and distribution money and assets to others.

Appendix II

Annotated Bibliography

Table of Categories for the Annotated Bibliography

ADVANCE DIRECTIVES
ADVOCACY
AFTERLIFE
AGING
AGING PARENTS
ASSISTED SUICIDE
BIOETHICS
BUDDHIST PERSPECTIVES
CAREGIVING
CHILDREN
COMMUNICATION
COMMUNITY
CREATIVITY
CREATIVE EXPRESSION
DENIAL
DYING & DEATH OVERVIEWS
DYING PROCESS
EDUCATION
EUTHANASIA
FINANCIAL & LEGAL ISSUES
FUNERALS
GRIEF

HOSPICE (see PALLIATIVE CARE & HOSPICE)
LESSONS FROM ILLNESS & DYING
MEDICAL CHOICES
ORGAN & TISSUE DONATION
PALLIATIVE CARE & HOSPICE
PERSONAL STORIES
PURPOSE IN LIFE
REINCARNATION
SPIRITUAL ISSUES

NOTES: When applicable, each category lists BOOKS, ORGANIZATIONS, and OTHER MEDIA (Booklet and Pamphlet; Audio-Tape and CD; Video and DVD). When a listing appears in more than one category, only the first listing will carry the annotation.

ADVANCE DIRECTIVES

BOOKS
Orman, Suze
The 9 Steps to Financial Freedom: Practical and Spiritual Steps So You Can Stop Worrying
New York: Crown, 1997
For advance directives, see chapter Four, "Being Responsible to Those You Love."

Quill, MD, Timothy E.
Death and Dignity: Making Choices and Taking Charge
New York: W.W. Norton, 1993
See chapters Nine, Ten, and Appendix. Information provided on advance directives is enhanced by discussions with patients regarding end-of-life choices.

ORGANIZATIONS
Aging with Dignity
PO Box 1661, Tallahassee, FL 32302
(888) 594-7437. *www.agingwithdignity.org*
Created the Five Wishes advance directive, that is less formal, more user-friendly, and with more choices than a standard Durable Power of Attorney for Health Care. Five Wishes may be downloaded from the website or ordered by mail. The site also notes which states approve it as a legal document.

Choice in Dying
200 Varick Street, 10th Floor, NY, NY 10014
(800) 989-9455. *www.choiceindying.org*
Created the first advance directive in 1967. The document may be downloaded from their website.

Last Acts Partnership: Advocating Quality End-of-Life Care (formerly *Partnership for Caring* and *Last Acts.*)
1620 Eye Street NW, Suite 202, Washington, DC 20006
(800) 989-9455. *www.lastacts.org*
Focuses on consumers through advocacy with professional and consumer organizations, grassroots, and individual partners. Also available: some direct services, such as a 24/7 hotline and advance directive forms.

Medic Alert.
2323 Colorado Avenue, Turlock, CA 95302
(888) 633-4298
Produces jewelry displaying a specific medical condition—diabetes, allergy—or a request, such as "DNR." When an emergency occurs in which the person cannot speak for herself, the jewelry informs emergency medical technicians of the condition. It also provides a toll free number for anyone to call their 24-hour Emergency Response Center.

US Living Will
PO Box 2789, Westfield, NJ 07091
(800) 548-9455. *www.uslivingwillregistry.com*
Provides electronic storage for your advance directives. These can be retrieved by your health care provider from anywhere in the country via

an automated computer-facsimile system.

OTHER MEDIA
Protection Portfolio (CD)
Orman, Suze
www.suzeorman.com.
Contains over 40 usable forms, including will, trust, advance directive, and financial power of attorney.

Who Will Speak for Robert? The Importance of Having an Advance Care Directive. (Video)
Produced by Center for Humane and Ethical Medical Care (CHEC√)
1250 16th Street, Santa Monica, CA 90404
(310) 319-4189.
Portrays the tragic and true story of Robert Wendland and his family. His truck accident produced severe brain damage requiring tube feeding. After many months his wife and teenage daughter decided to remove the tube, which was his expressed, but not written, wish. The mother opposed the wife in court and won. The lawyers, doctors, and ethicists interviewed in this case agree that a written advance directive by Robert probably would have spared him and his family from eight years of suffering.

ADVOCACY

ORGANIZATIONS
*AARP (*Formerly known as *American Association for Retired Persons)*
601 E Street NW, Washington, DC 20049
(800) 424-3410. *www.aarp.org*
AARP serves as the largest advocacy organization for many issues related to elders: health care, Social Security, legal problems, political change, and housing. Encouragement and instructions are provided for helping to create change. Monthly newsletter and magazine.

Americans for Better Care of the Dying
4200 Wisconsin Avenue NW, 4th Floor, Washington, DC 20016
(202) 895-2660. w*ww.abcd-caring.org*
Mission: To ensure that Americans can count on good end-of-life care by
building momentum for reform; exploring new methods and systems for
delivering care; and shaping public policy through evidence-based
understanding. Focuses on fundamental reforms, such as improved pain
management, better financial reimbursement systems, enhanced continuity
of care, support for family caregivers, and changes in public policy.

Capitol Advantage
2751 Prosperity Avenue, Suite 600, Fairfax, VA 22031
(800) 659-8708. *www.capwiz.com*
A grassroots legislative action tool. By typing in your zip code, you receive
a listing of your political representatives and their contact information,
party, legislation, and more.

*Last Acts Partnership: Advocating Quality End-of-Life Care (*formerly,
  Partnership for Caring and Last Acts.)
(See annotation under ADVANCE DIRECTIVES.)

AFTER-LIFE

BOOKS
Darling, David
Soul Search: A Scientist Explores the Afterlife
New York: Villard Books, 1995
The author looks at death and dying from a scientific point of view: the
brain holds our being-ness and therefore, when it is dead, we are dead. He
utilizes ideas drawn from quantum physics, age-old philosophers and
mystics, and drug and meditation experiences. Then, he concludes, the
death of the brain finally allows us to become who we really are: timeless
consciousness, intimately reunited with all of nature, and freed from
isolation.

Hatch, Judge David Patterson (channeled through Elsa Barker)
Letters from the Light: An Afterlife Journal from the Self-Lighted World

Originally published in 1914
Edited by Kathy Hart
Oregon: Beyond Words Publishing, 1997
Fifty-two delightful mini-chapters describe an educated, thoughtful, and wise person's experiences "on the other side." David Hatch was a superior court judge in Santa Barbara in the late 1800's; Elsa Barker was a friend.

Hart writes, "One does not have to believe in channeling to appreciate the wisdom so eloquently put forth by the writer...[Hatch and Barker] provide an inspirational perspective on death and life, that both mitigates our fears of dying and compels us to live life to the fullest."

Miller, PhD, Sukie
After Death: How People Around the World Map the Journey After Life
New York: Simon & Schuster, 1997
A psychologist specializing in work with the terminally ill, Miller developed a great interest in the mythologies and cosmologies of people in different cultures. She created the Institute for the Study of the Afterdeath, and from there gathered stories and experiences documenting the differences and commonalities of the ways in which people hold the "after-dfeath."

Moody, Jr., MD, Raymond A.
Life After Life
New York: Bantam Books, 1988
This landmark book tells stories of people who had been pronounced "clinically dead" and survived to tell their experiences. Their testimonies of death and beyond were similar and positive. Many found their lives to be changed markedly after the "near-death experiences."

Peck, MD, M. Scott
In Heaven as on Earth: A Vision of the Afterlife
New York: Hyperion, 1996
"It can be read in several ways. It is a stirring work of imagination—a novel that gives us a fascinating view of what the afterlife may bring; and it is also a profound book about the self—a book in which we come to see that Dr. Peck's vision of how to thrive in the afterlife can teach us important things about living our own lives here on Earth."

AGING

BOOKS
Carter, Jimmy
The Virtues of Aging
New York: Ballantine, 2000
Carter urges older Americans to take charge of their lives by staying active whether through volunteerism or personal recreation; to rely on oneself as much as possible; to get involved with others; and to put one's affairs in order with the awareness that all lives will end.

Hillman, James
The Force of Character and the Lasting Life
New York: Ballantine, 1999
This book "...follows an enriching journey through the three stages of aging—lasting, the deepening that comes with longevity; leaving, the preparation for departure; and left, the special legacy we each bestow on our survivors. Along the way the book explores the meanings and often hidden virtues of characteristic physical and emotional changes, such as loss of memory, alterations in sleep patterns, and the mysterious upsurge in erotic imagination."

Ram Dass
Still Here: Embracing Aging, Changing, and Dying
New York: Penguin Putnam, 2000
"Ram Dass helps us explore the joy, pain, and opportunities of the ripening seasons of our lives. Writing with his trademark humor and wisdom, sharing stories from his own life, and meditation exercises to integrate the teachings into daily life, Ram Dass offers us a new perspective on the territory that lies ahead. It is a perspective on aging, changing, and dying that he hopes will make the tumultuous process a little easier for all of us."

AGING PARENTS

BOOKS
Ilardo, Joseph A.
As Parents Age: A Psychological and Practical Guide
Acton, MA: VanderWyk & Burnham, 1998
Down to earth advice that considers many aspects of adult children relating to elderly parents, as well as to those giving care to an elder neighbor or friend.

Illardo, Joseph A. with Carole R. Rothman
Are Your Parents Driving you Crazy?: How to Resolve the Most
  Common Dilemmas with Aging Parents
Acton, MA: VanderWyk & Burnham, 2001
Discusses such familiar topics as: a parent who refuses to stop driving, seeing a doctor, discussing end-of-life issues, or when a parent wants to move in with you. Also, deals with other family members who don't offer to help, or who resent the time you spend with your parent.

Marcell, Jacqueline
Elder Rage—or—Take My Father...Please!: How to Survive Caring for
  Aging Parents
Irvine, CA: Impressive Press, 2000
A personal story, written with compassion and humor, about the frustrations and the solutions of caring for a difficult parent. Includes how to get: a correct diagnosis, the proper medications, behavior modification techniques for handling difficult elders, and valuable advice and resources to make caring for your loved one easier.

Pipher, Mary
Another Country: Navigating the Emotional Terrain of Our Elders
New York: Penguin Putnam, 1999
Pipher describes the increasingly complex and difficult relationships experienced between elders and their children. She presents new ways of supporting our parents and grandparents with our time, energy, and love. In turn, we will learn how to prepare for our own aging process.

ASSISTED SUICIDE (see EUTHANASIA)

BIOETHICS

BOOKS
Callahan, Daniel
Setting Limits: Medical Goals in an Aging Society
Reprint with a new afterword
Washington, DC: Georgetown University Press, 1987 and 1995
A provocative, intelligent, and well-researched look at the growing number of the elderly in relation to medical progress and its cost to our society. Callahan urges that we begin now, before this population's care becomes a full-blown crisis, to examine our expectations of elder care in the future. He suggests we examine two controversial notions: first, that we should try to modernize old age and turn it into a permanent middle age; and second, that there should be no limits to the claims of the elderly to expensive life-extending medicine under public entitlement programs.

___. *The Troubled Dream of Life: In Search of a Peaceful Death* Washington, DC: Georgetown University Press, 2000
"Drawing on his own experience, and on literature, philosophy, and medicine, Callahan offers great insight into how to deal with the rewards of modern medicine without upsetting our equilibrium and perspective on dying. By examining the way we view death and the care of the dying and critically ill, Callahan's perspective greatly enhances the legal and moral discussions about end-of-life issues."

Caplan, Arthur
Am I My Brother's Keeper?: The Ethical Frontiers of Biomedicine
Indiana University Press, 1998
The author, director for the Center of Bioethics at the University of Pennsylvania, gets to the heart of such issues as assisted suicide, cloning, abortion, and organ transplants. Caplan emphasizes the notion of trust and the need for professional groups to work through ethical dilemmas. He echoes a resounding "yes" to the question posed in his title.

ORGANIZATIONS

Nursing Ethics Network (NEN)
www.nursingethcisnetwork.org

An organization that gives nurses a high-tech way to solve ethical dilemmas and access the latest ethics resources. Nurses can visit the NEN's website to submit their ethics questions, which are then referred to one of the 20 members of the network's advisory board—composed of nursing professionals with expertise in areas such as end-of-life issues, nursing ethics, and palliative care. They are careful not to give answers to the questions but provide the resources to help a nurse find her own solution.

National Reference Center for Bioethical Literature
Kennedy Institute of Ethics
Georgetown University, PO Box 571212, Washington, DC 20057
(800) 246-3849. *www.bioethics.georgetown.edu*

Provides access to library resources concerned with ethical issues: bibliographies, links, organizations, and teaching resources.

BUDDHIST PERSPECTIVES

BOOKS

Dalai Lama, His Holiness the
Advice on Dying and Living a Better Life
Translated and edited by Jeffrey Hopkins, PhD
New York: Atria Books, 2002

The Dalai Lama shows us how to prepare for death and in doing so, how to enrich our time on earth and die without fear or upset.

____. *The Joy of Living and Dying in Peace*
New York: HarperCollins, 1997

"A treasury of simple wisdom: a primer for living with purpose and for dying in peace. His Holiness the Dalai Lama presents his own luminous thoughts and comforting guidance, and draws upon the wisdom of Buddhist tradition as he expands our understanding of the end of life— and of what it means to be 'prepared'."

Levine, Stephen
A Year to Live: How to Live This Year as if It Were Your Last
New York: Doubleday, 1997
"Most of us go to extraordinary lengths to ignore, laugh off, or deny the fact that we are going to die, but preparing for death is one of the most rational and rewarding acts of a lifetime. It is an exercise that gives us the opportunity to deal with unfinished business and enter into a new and vibrant relationship with life. Levine provides us with a year-long program of intensely practical strategies and powerful guided meditations to help with this work, so that whenever the ultimate moment does arrive for each of us, we will not feel that it has come too soon."

Longaker, Christine
Facing Death and Finding Hope
New York: Doubleday, 1997
If you have not read or studied Buddhist philosophy on death and dying, this book is an informative and easy place to start. Christine Longaker's introduction to dying and Buddhism came to her after the death of her young husband. She studied with Sogyal Rinpoche and now teaches throughout the United States and abroad. She helped establish the Hospice of Santa Cruz County in California. The book is readable, compassionate, very user-friendly, and includes the explanation of the "Four Tasks of Living and Dying," as well as specific advice for caregivers, parents, and survivors of the dying.

Rinpoche, Sogyal
The Tibetan Book of Living and Dying
San Francisco: Harper, 1994
"...a manual for life and death and a magnificent source of sacred inspiration from the heart of the Tibetan tradition. Sogyal Rinpoche delivers a lucid and inspiring introduction to the practice of mediation, to the nature of mind, to karma and rebirth, to compassionate love and care for the dying, and to the trials and rewards of the spiritual path."

Rosenberg, Larry
Living in the Light of Death: On the Art of Being Truly Alive
Boston and London: Shambala, 2000
"An invaluable primer for virtually anyone who has a body and is old

enough to read. Larry Rosenberg dives right to the core of what it takes to be truly alive and, with the lightest and kindest of touches, shows us simple ways to wake up to our lives while we have them to live. A true vehicle for exploring the profound question of whether there is life before death."

Thich Nhat Hanh
No Death No Fear: Comforting Wisdom for Life
New York: Riverhead Books, 2002
Addressing the human fear of nothingness after death, the author explains how readers can conquer fears and live happier lives through a close examination of who we are and how we live.

OTHER MEDIA
Sounds True. (Audio tapes and CDs.)
413 S. Arthur Avenue, Louisville, CO 80306
(800) 333-9185. *www.soundstrue.com*
Free catalogue contains recordings of many of the teachers listed above, including Ram Dass, Pema Chodrun, Thich Nhat Hanh, as well as *The Tibetan Book of the Dead.*

CAREGIVING (also see HOSPICE)

BOOKS
Capossela, Cappy, and Sheila Warnock
Share the Care: How to Organize a Group to Care for Someone Who Is Seriously Ill
New York: Simon & Schuster, 1995
The authors provide valuable guidelines, compassionate suggestions, and a simple-to-use workbook section that together offer support to help free the patient from worry and the caregivers from burnout. Here is the best answer to the question, "What can I do?"

Lynn, MD, Joanne, and Joan Harrold, MD.
Handbook for Mortals: Guidance for People Facing Serious Illness
New York: Oxford University Press, 1999
If you are faced with a seriously ill family member or friend, this book will

help you gather all the resources you need. How to cope with the uncertainty of illness, orchestrate support, have conversations with the doctor, manage symptoms and pain, and make difficult end-of-life decisions.

Marcell, Jacqueline
Elder Rage—or—Take my Father Please!: How to Survive Caring for Aging Parents
(See annotation under AGING PARENTS.)

McLeod, Beth Witrogen
Caregiving: The Spiritual Journey of Love, Loss, and Renewal
New York: John Wiley & Sons, 1999
An indispensable guide for anyone who is, was, or may become a caregiver. *Caregiving* includes advice from leaders in the fields of aging, medicine, finance, and spirituality. The book explores medical and financial problems, depression, stress, housing, home care, and end-of-life concerns.

Nouwen, Henri J.M
Our Greatest Gift: A Meditation on Dying and Caring
New York: Harper Collins, 1994
A Catholic priest and eloquent writer, the author challenges us to accept our death as part of our spiritual journey, not its end. He reveals the gifts that the dying give to one another through acceptance and caring.

Waxman, Stephanie
A Helping Hand: When a Loved One is Critically Ill
Los Angeles: Marco Press, 2000
(888) 242-6608. *www.wisdomoftheworld.com*
This small, simple and thoughtful workbook helps family members and friends deal with the strong and overwhelming emotions that arise during a medical crisis. Examples are given to promote understanding, foster endurance, and inspire hope.

ORGANIZATIONS
AccentCare
(800) 834-3059. *www.accentcare.com*
One of the nation's leading personal in-home care services, this site now

offers a free on-line resource for implementing an eldercare strategy. Based on your responses to a survey, the site will tell you the most appropriate level of care. From there, you can check out directories of services and supplies.

Americans for Better Care of the Dying.
(See annotation under ADVOCACY.)

California Partnership for Long-Term Care
Mail Stop 4100, PO Box 942732
Sacramento, CA 94234
(800) 227-3445. *www.dhs.ca.gov/cpltc*
Their mission is to provide Californians with affordable long-term care insurance protection so they will not have to spend everything they have worked for on LTC.

CareGuide
12301 NW 39th Street, Coral Springs, FL 33065
(888) 389-8839. *www.careguide.com*
One of the best sites on the Internet for understanding what in-home and outside-facility care costs and how to plan for both. It also offers a handy search engine that can help identify local home-care, assisted living, and nursing home facilities.

Eden Alternative. Summer Hill Company
742 Turnpike Road, Sherburne, NY 13460
(607) 674-5232. *www.edenalt.com*
A new way to care for the elderly in environments rich with children, plants, and animals. The website describes the principles, trainings, and locations now in existence.

ElderWeb
1305 Chadwick Drive, Normal, IL 61761
(309) 451-3319. *www.elderweb.com*
Like CareGuide, this site provides a good overview of regional resources for all phases of care. Includes local directories of aging and health organizations, nursing homes, assisted living facilities, and other care programs and services.

Last Acts Partnership: Advocating Quality End-of-Life Care (formerly
   Partnership for Caring and *Last Acts)*
(See annotation under ADVANCE DIRECTIVES.)

Life Line
(800) 543-3546. *www.lifelinesys.com*
For over thirty years, the system has provided personal emergency response
services: by pushing a button on a necklace or bracelet, LifeLine is reached
and proceeds with the appropriate response to the caller's needs, such as
calling an ambulance, a neighbor, or family member.

National Association for Home Care
228 7th Street SE, Washington, DC 20003
(202) 547-7424. *www.nahc.org*
NAHC is the nation's largest trade association representing the interests
and concerns of home-care agencies, hospices, home-care aide
organizations, and medical equipment suppliers. They provide current
information regarding professional development and advocate for better
state and federal regulations concerning hospice and home care.

National Shared Housing Resource Center, Rita Zadoff
5342 Tilly Mill Road, Dunwoody, CA 30338
(770) 395-2625. *www.nationalsharedhousing.org*
For a growing number of Americans faced with losing their independence,
shared housing is an affordable and viable alternative. A home sharer might
be a senior citizen, a person with disabilities, a homeless person, a single
parent, an AIDS patient, or simply a person wishing to share his or her life
with others. Shared housing offers companionship, security, mutual
support, and more. See website for regional directors.

OTHER MEDIA
And Thou Shalt Honor. (Video, DVD)
www.andthoushalthonor.com
A two-hour original broadcast first aired on PBS in March, 2002. An
outstanding guide for family caregivers, present and future. May be ordered
along with its companion book from the website.

On Our Own Terms: Moyers on Dying in America (Video.)
www.pbs.org/wnet/onourownterms/
Bill Moyer's landmark television production on end-of-life care (first aired on PBS in September, 2000). A useful tool for educating and encouraging discussion about end-of-life issues. Available from the website.

CHILDREN

BOOKS
Buscaglia, PhD, Leo
The Fall of Freddie the Leaf: A Story of Life for All Ages
Thorofare, NJ: Slack Incorporated, 1982
Like humans, leaves have purpose, grow, change their physical nature, and finally die. This analogy, along with beautiful photographs, provides children and adults a way to discuss life and death in a realistic way.

Han, Carolyn Everett
Kalapana
Honolulu, HI: Island Heritage Publishing, 1999
Written for children (and grown children) to process grief by learning that life is circular: "...nothing ever dies—it only changes form." A cat flees the lava of an erupting volcano, survives, and is adopted by a Hawaiian girl. Exquisitely illustrated and flavored by Hawaiian lore.

Hanson, Warren
The Next Place
Minneapolis, MN: Waldman House Press, 1997
This beautifully illustrated book shifts the focus from "dying" to the "passing of life." It increases comfort regarding death for children and adults.

Knapp, Ronald, J.
Beyond Endurance: When a Child Dies
New York: Schocken Books, 1986
Perhaps no event is as traumatic as the death of a child. Knapp interviewed 155 families who had experienced such a loss to determine how they coped, or failed to cope, with the tragedy. He suggests specific ways in

which families can deal with three types of death: death occurring after a long illness; sudden or unexpected death—usually by accident; and death by murder. Each presents different problems in the mourning process.

Mundy, Michaelene
Sad Isn't Bad: A Good-Grief Guidebook for Kids Dealing with Loss
Illustrated by R.W. Alley
St. Meinrad, IN: One Caring Place, Abbey Press, 1998
Children of all ages and their families will find a comforting and realistic look at loss, along with positive, life-affirming help for coping with loss as a child. The book promotes honest and healthy grief and growth.

COMMUNICATION

BOOKS
Kessler, David
The Rights of the Dying
New York: HarperCollins Publishers, 1997
"In a gentle, compassionate language, David Kessler outlines the seventeen rights of the dying, principles that will help people face death with dignity. For family members, the book provides a vocabulary, a way of communicating with one another, as well as with doctors and hospital staff. It also provides a way of allowing the dying family member to participate in all decisions and express his or her own feelings and emotions."

Zimmerman, Jack, and Virginia Coyle
The Way of Council
Las Vegas, NV: Bramble Books, 1996
This comprehensive book describes the history and method of using council as a way of communication between groups (large and small), couples, families, classrooms and businesses. It provides a valuable method for discussing end-of-life issues.

ORGANIZATIONS
Center for Living Council: The Ojai Foundation
9739 Ojai-Santa Paula Road
Ojai, CA 93023

(805) 646-8343. *www.ojaifoundation.org*
Dedicated to the Way of Council. (See above: BOOKS, Zimmerman.) Honoring spiritual practice in all traditions, service to others, and stewardship of the land. Teachers learn the method of using council and how to take council out into the larger community.

Association of Personal Historians
870 NW 178th Avenue, Beaverton, OR 97006
(503) 645-0616. *www.personalhistorians.org*
Members are dedictated to helping others to preserve their personal histories and life stories.

COMMUNITY

BOOKS
Metzger, Deena
Entering the Ghost River: Meditations on the Theory and Practice
   of Healing
Topanga, CA: Hand to Hand Press, 2003
"Deena brings her knowledge and experience of healing body and soul to the issues of healing community, both locally and globally. Following the threads of September 11th, she shows us how we can understand the larger story, and awaken to ourselves. This awakening and alleviation of suffering comes through the context of kinship, of community, of Story."

Shaffer, Carolyn, and Kristin Anundsen
Creating Community Anywhere: Finding Support and Connection in a
   Fragmented World
New York: Jeremy P. Tarcher, 1993
"If you dream of more emotional encouragement and practical support in your life, of more aliveness and fulfillment in your contact with others...this book...tells you how to create it. Whether you live in an urban or rural area, are single or married, reside near or far from your family, you will find the many opportunities explored here to be exciting sources of community."

ORGANIZATIONS

L'Arche USA
(503) 282-6231. *www.larcheusa.org*
"People are yearning to discover community. We have had enough of loneliness, independence and competition." Jean Vanler.

Cohousing Association of the United States
1504 Franklin Street, Suite 102, Oakland, CA 94612
(510) 844-0865. *www.cohousing.org*
The organization promotes and encourages the cohousing concept, supports both individuals and groups in creating communities, and provides networking opportunities for those involved or interested in cohousing.

National Shared Housing Resource Center
(See annotation under CAREGIVING.)

Rallying Points
6620 Eye Street, Suite 202, Washington, DC 20006
(800) 341-0050. *www.rallyingpoints.org*
When Bill Moyers and his team prepared On Our Own Terms in 2000, they encouraged communities across the US to create coalitions working to improve end-of-life care. Rallying Points connects these coalitions with each other. It encourages them to identify community needs for better care of the dying, advocate for health system changes, and develop specific projects that support dying people and their families.

Wellness Community—National
10921 Reed Hartman Highway, Suite 215, Cincinnati, OH 45242
(888) 793-9355. *www.thewellnesscommunity.org*
A national organization composed of over fifty local centers. People with cancer and their families can be with others to build support and reduce feelings of loneliness. Support groups, education, and counseling are available.

OTHER RESOURCES
How to find directories or locations of community caregiving and senior services.

Check your local senior or community center for a guidebook or directory that lists resources related to caregiving in your area. These publications are a valuable tool when you need residential care, aid, day care or transportation.

For examples of directories, contact: City of Santa Monica Commission on Older Americans, 1527 4th Street, Room 106, Santa Monica, CA 90401; or mail $4 for a directory to UCLA Center on Aging, 10945 Le Conte Avenue, Suite 319, Los Angeles, CA 90095. (310) 794-0676.
For an example of a location within a community that provides multiple services related to health, healing, education, support, and dying well (or for ideas to create a center in your area) contact: Beach Cities Health District. 514 N. Prospect Avenue, Redondo Beach, CA 90277. (310) 374-3426. *www.bchd.org*

CREATIVITY

BOOKS
Cameron, Julia
The Artist's Way
New York: Jeremy P. Tarcher, 1992
Cameron provides a comprehensive program to recover creativity from self-limiting beliefs such as fear, sabotage, and guilt, based on the principle that creative expression is the natural direction of life. The writing exercises are very useful in processing end-of-life issues, as well as getting through day-to-day difficulties with ill family members or long-term caregiving situations.

ORGANIZATIONS
Toastmasters International
PO Box 9052, Mission Viejo, CA 92690
(949) 858-1207. *www.toastmasters.org*
For over sixty years, Toastmasters has helped people quell their fears of public speaking, as well as develop leadership skills. It is a valuable tool to help reader's of this book become advocates for the many changes needed to improve end-of-life care and increase the comfort with which we discuss dying and death.

CREATIVE EXPRESSIONS ABOUT DYING AND DEATH

BOOKS
Anaya, Rudolfo.
Bless Me Ultima
Berkeley, CA: TQS Publications, 1972
An award-winning novel of a young boy's experience of life and death in New Mexico as he is guided by the wise old woman, Ultima.

Coelho, Paulo
Veronika Decides to Die
New York: HarperCollins, 1998
In this novel, a young woman attempts suicide and awakens in a mental hospital in her native Slovenia. The awareness that she was unsuccessful, plus the news that she damaged her heart, provide a dramatic setting for her examination of the meaning of life and death. In addition, the other inmates are affected by her situation and begin wondering what they can learn and how they might change.

Tolstoy, Leo
"The Death of Ivan Ilych," *The Death of Ivan Ilych and Other Stories*
New York: Penguin Books, 1960
Although this short story was written over a hundred years ago, the brilliant and prolific author touches on the same issues around death and dying that we are faced with today: self-deception, denial, wrong diagnoses, pain, wondering if the life was well-lived, and rage. In only sixty pages, we learn about the life of Ivan Ilych and his tormented dying process.

MOVIES
Afterlife
Directed by Kore-ed Hirozaku. English subtitles.
Japan, 1998
People who have recently died are received in a school-like way station. They are told they will have a few days to choose one cherished memory from their lifetime that they will carry with them into eternity. This engaging film explores the need to discover meaning in everyday life.

Antonia's Line
Directed by Marleen Gorris. English subtitles.
Netherlands, 1995
Antonia wakes up one morning believing it will be the last day of her life. She decides to call her family together to say good-bye and asks her great-granddaughter, who is drawn to the mysteries of death, to remain with her until the last moment. Antonia then recalls her life—shown as a kind of life review—as she waits for her farewell gathering.

Children of Nature
Directed by Fridrik Thor Fridriksson. English subtitles.
Iceland, 1991
An elderly farmer, marooned in an old folks' home in Reykjavik, discovers that his childhood sweetheart is also living there. While reminiscing about their youth, they decide to run away to their hometown in the remote west fjords. With a small amount of savings and new running shoes, the pair sets off on their adventure. Nominated for Best Foreign Film Academy Award of 1991, *Children of Nature* explores the seductive idea that, for those near the end of life, a state of grace can be achieved through a reunion with nature and a sense of place.

Innocence
Directed by Paul Cox.
Australia, 2001
A man and woman in their seventies reunite after forty years of separation. A love affair develops in the face of nearing death. Touching conversations take place between them about love, life, and death, while their families react to the relationship.

Iris
Directed by Richard Eyre
Starring Judi Dench and Jim Broadbent as the aging Iris and John, and Kate Winslet and Hugh Bonneville as the couple during their youth. Based on the book *Elegy for Iris* by John Bayley.
USA, Miramax, 2002
Tells the inspiring and heartbreaking story of Bayley's forty-year marriage with English novelist and philosopher, Dame Iris Murdoch. Their youthful romance, brilliant minds, and professional successes are made all the more

poignant as Iris declines from Alzheimer's. In their last years together, John tries to take care of her, often with painful and pathetic results.

John Q
Directed by Nick Cassavetes.
Starring Denzel Washington.
USA, 2002.
A boy needs an emergency heart transplant to stay alive. His father, John Q. Archibald, played by Washington, finds his health insurance won't cover the surgery, the hospital won't provide special assistance, and the child is left to die. The film turns into a gripping suspense thriller while it examines and brings to light the cost of transplants and how selection processes for recipients might be made.

Last Orders
Directed by Fred Schepisi.
Starring Michael Caine, Bob Hoskins, Helen Mirren.
Based on the Booker Prize-winning novel by Graham Swift.
Sony Pictures Classics, USA, 2002
As they take their recently departed friend's ashes to the sea, four buddies from South London review their intertwined lives over a half century. Following his "last orders," the long drive with frequent pub stops allows deep reflections on life and death, love and loss.

My Life Without Me
Directed by Isabel Coixet.
USA, 2003
A young woman is diagnosed with terminal cancer and decides she will not tell her husband, two daughters, and mother about her illness. This tender and thought-provoking film provides a brave look at one possibility of dealing with impending death.

One True Thing
Directed by Carl Franklin.
Starring Meryl Streep, William Hurt, and Renee Zellweger.
Based on the book by Anna Quindlen. USA, 1998
An intimate look at how one family copes with and confronts cancer and death, and possibly, assisted-suicide. The points of view of each family

member allow the viewer to explore the different reactions and multiple feelings that occur in such a situation.

Philadelphia
Directed by Jonathan Demme.
Starring Tom Hanks and Denzel Washington.
USA, 1994
Two competing lawyers join forces to sue a prestigious law firm for AIDS discrimination, as Hanks' character is dying from AIDS. Honor, rage, heartbreak, and astonishing humor shine through this difficult story.

Ponette
Directed by Jacques Doillon. English subtitles.
France, 1997
A four-year-old child suffers the loss of her parents. The film tracks her sensitive responses to her new surroundings with her cousins, her moments alone, and her emergence from grief.

Straight Story, The
Directed by David Lynch.
Starring Richard Farnsworth and Sissy Spacek.
USA, 1999
Based on a true story, Alvin Straight sets out on his John Deere lawn mower, traveling 260 miles to make amends with his estranged brother, who had recently suffered a stroke. The film follows this poignant six-week journey, Alvin's inner thoughts, his outer conversations with the people he meets, and his perseverance in accomplishing his goal of forgiveness.

Wit
Directed by Mike Nichols.
Starring Emma Thompson.
Based on Margaret Edson's stage play, winner of the 1999 Pulitzer Prize.
HBO, USA, 2002
A brilliant English professor who has lived through words and wit is diagnosed with advanced ovarian cancer. Throughout eight months of severe treatment, she intellectually examines her reactions to life, finally accessing her feelings because of the tenderness of her nurse and a visit from a colleague who climbs into her bed to offer comfort. The difficult

issues related to technology and caregiving are beautifully illustrated. See p. 247 for information on the "Wit" Film Project.

MUSIC
Graceful Passages: A Companion for Living and Dying. (2 CD set with 56-page gift book).
Companion Arts, PO Box 2528, Novato, CA 94948
(888) 242-6608. *www.wisdomoftheworld.com*
Composed and played by Michael Stillwater and Gary Remal Malkin. The first CD provides an opportunity for the listener to both relax and be supported in freely expressing feelings, which will lead to reconciliation, resolution, and peaceful transitions. The second CD presents foremost experts in the field of dying and death who speak candidly about the key elements of the dying process. Accompanied by music.

Chalice of Repose Project, Inc.
PO Box 169, Mt. Angel, OR 97362
www.music-thanatologyassociation.com
The word "thanatology" comes from the Greek word for death, thanatos. Music Thanatology is a field in which practitioners provide musical comfort, using harp, voice, and a special repertoire of music, at the bedside of patients near the end of life. The service at the bedside is called a "music vigil" and is delivered by one or two highly trained music-thanatologists. Its purpose is to lovingly serve the needs of the dying and their loved ones with calming, transformational music.

DENIAL

BOOKS
Becker, Ernest
The Denial of Death
New York: Simon & Schuster, 1973
This Pulitzer Prize-winner often receives gracious credit from other authors writing about dying and death. Becker explores western psychology and philosophy for clues as to why we deny death, and what that denial causes in our culture. Through this study, "we are beginning to acknowledge that the bitter medicine he prescribes—contemplation of the

horror of our inevitable death—is, paradoxically, the tincture that adds sweetness to mortality."

Reading Dr. Becker's reflections on Freud, Kierkegaard and Rank, among others, not only illuminates the steps Westerners have taken to avoid thinking about death and why, but also amplifies and explains the work of these important schools of thought over the last 150 years.

ORGANIZATIONS
The Ernest Becker Foundation
3621 72nd Street, Mercer Island, WA 98040
http://faculty.washington.edu/nelgee/aboutebf/default.htm
The mission of the foundation is to cultivate and support scholarly works that explore and extend Becker's insights. They also publish a newsletter and organize lectures and conferences based on his work.

DYING AND DEATH OVERVIEWS

BOOKS
Jones, Constance
R.I.P.: The Complete Book of Death & Dying
New York: HarperCollins, 1997
Traditions, statistics, amusing stories, facts and practical information. Everything you didn't even know you wanted to know.

Kübler-Ross, MD, Elisabeth
On Death and Dying
New York: Macmillan Publishing Company, 1969
The quintessential book that first alerted the public to the need of talking about death and dying with our loved ones. Includes Kübler-Ross's stages of dying—denial, isolation, anger, bargaining, depression, and acceptance—that have become landmarks in this field.

___. *Death, The Final Stage of Growth*
New York: Simon & Schuster, 1975
"Drawing on our own and other cultures' views of death and dying, Kübler-Ross provides some illuminating answers to the questions: Why do

we treat death as a taboo? What are the sources of our fears? How do we express our grief? How do we accept the death of a person close to us? How can we prepare for our own death? She offers a spectrum of viewpoints, including those of ministers, rabbis, doctors, nurses, and sociologists, and the personal accounts of those near death and their survivors."

Webb, Marilyn
The Good Death: The New American Search to Reshape the End of Life
New York: Bantam Books, 1997
Meticulously researched and annotated, Webb's book provides an important overview of the path many Americans are taking to create better end-of-life care. The author explores hospice care, assisted suicide, actual supreme court sessions, workshops with Kübler-Ross, and interviews with families who have used the services of Dr. Kervorkian. She also includes many real-life scenarios of people undergoing the most difficult passages to the most conscious and peaceful.

DYING PROCESS

BOOKS
Kessler, David. *The Rights of the Dying.* (See annotation under
COMMUNICATION.)

Kothari, MD, Manu L., and Lope A. Mehta, MD
Death: A New Perspective in the Phenomena of Disease and Dying
London: Marion Boyars Publishers, 1986
Contains a detailed investigation of medical attitudes and practices relating to the terminally ill and the inevitability of death. The authors are severely critical of the medical establishment's arrogant, misguided desire to abolish death by trying to preserve life at all costs. This, they argue, is outside the scope of the true function of caring for the sick and has had many damaging consequences, especially the fixation with technological hardware and lack of respect or reverence for the experiences of dying. These conditions result from a failure to deal with the deeper questions concerning the quality of life, both for those who die and those who live on.

Lynch, Thomas
The Undertaking: Life Studies from the Dismal Trade
New York: W.W. Norton & Company, 1997
A witty and deep read about death and dying from a man who is both a poet and an undertaker. He tells the stories of his clients as well as his own family. He urges us to look at life and death in many different ways, bringing an artful and poetic view to what has been called the "Dismal Trade."

Nuland, MD, Sherwin B.
How We Die: Reflections on Life's Final Chapter
New York: Random House, 1995
Nuland describes the physiological processes by which people most often die, including heart disease, Alzheimer's, accidents, suicide, euthanasia, AIDS, cancer, and viral attacks. His portrayal of patients and their situations is descriptive, understandable, and extremely compassionate. It is also of value in teaching us more about how our bodies work when they are well.

Tobin, MD, Daniel R. with Karen Lindsey
Peaceful Dying: The Step-by-Step Guide to Preserving Your Dignity, Your Choice, and Your Inner Peace at the End of Life
New York: HarperCollins Publishers, 1999
Daniel Tobin has created the FairCare Health System. This plan teaches health systems and managed-care organizations to provide patients and their families the best possible end-of-life care.

EDUCATION

ORGANIZATIONS
"Wit" Film Project
Contact Jennifer Spooner
(310) 478-3711, ext.48353. *www.growthhouse.org/witfilmproject/*
The goal of the "Wit" Film Project is to enhance trainee education—in medical schools and hospitals—regarding the humanistic elements of end-of-life care. The dramatic presentation, starring Emma Thompson, evokes feelings that are difficult to access through other educational methods. Program materials are available to aid discussions for medical students,

interns and residents. See p. 243 for description of the film, *Wit*.

Facing the Final Mystery Workshop
Laura Larsen, RN
(818) 706-9814. *www.lauralarsen.com*
Since 1998, Laura has conducted workshops based on the material in this
book. The groups are small—ten to fifteen participants—allowing for
intimate sharing and learning with each other regarding end-of-life issues.
In California, the workshop provides CEUs for RNs, LSWs and MFTs.
She also lectures and teaches in other educational settings. Contact Laura
to set up a workshop or presentation in your town or workplace.

Upaya
1404 Cerro Gordo, Santa Fe, NM 87501
(505) 986-8518. *www.upaya.org*
Upaya means "craft of compassion" and is a Buddhist study center that
includes the Project on Being with Dying. Its purpose is to inspire a gentle
revolution in the relationship to dying and living by training health care
professionals who, in turn, bring contemplative work with dying people
back to their home institutions.

World University of America Ojai
PO Box 1567, Ojai, CA 93024
(805) 646-1444. *www.worldu.edu*
In addition to psychological counseling degrees, World University offers a
certificate in Thanatology (care for the dying) and presents an annual
seminar, The International Conference on Conscious Living and Dying.

EUTHANASIA (ASSISTED SUICIDE)

BOOKS
Humphrey, Derek
Final Exit: The Practicalities of Self-Deliverance and Assisted Suicide
  for the Dying
New York: Dell, 1992
Final Exit is the main publication of the *Hemlock Society* (now called *End-*

of-Life Choices), and describes in detail how a person can use legally prescribed medications to end life.

Peck, MD, M. Scott
Denial of the Soul
New York: Harmony Books, Crown Publishers, Inc., 1997
"Dr. Peck grapples with the deeper meanings of life, death, suicide, and euthanasia, and asks whether we have the ethical right to kill ourselves even though we have the power. How does taking a life differ from allowing death? Whose consent does euthanasia require: the patient's, the family's, or the government's? When does physical or emotional pain become a ground for euthanasia? What can we learn from the process of dying a natural death?"

Quill, MD, Timothy
Death and Dignity: Making Choices and Taking Charge
New York: W. W. Norton & Company, 1993
Quill bravely tells why he helped a long-time patient, stricken with leukemia, to take her life when her suffering became intolerable. While he feels that most people can die with dignity and without pain using comfort care methods, he admits there are those few who suffer deeply. He asks for regulation, rather than denial, of physician-assisted suicide.

ORGANIZATIONS
*End-of-Life Choices (*formerly, *The Hemlock Society)*
PO Box 101810, Denver, CO 80250
(800) 247-7421. *www.endoflifechoices.org*
Believes that people should be able to have choice and dignity at the end of life and the option of a peaceful, gentle, certain, and swift death in the company of their loved ones. The society has a legislative arm seeking laws to protect patients and physicians. Quarterly newsletter.

Hemlock Society, The.
(See *End-of-Life Choices*.)

FINANCIAL AND LEGAL ISSUES

BOOKS
Gentry, F. Bruce and Jens C. Appel III
The Complete Will Kit
New York: John Wiley & Sons, 1997
Contains legal information on how to write, rewrite, or revise your will; forms that help you do it yourself; the latest information as of date of publication, on living wills; and advice on power of attorney.

Orman, Suze
*The 9 Steps to Financial Freedom: Practical & Spiritual Steps So You
   Can Stop Worrying*
New York: Crown Publishers, 1997
This 1998-9 bestseller helps people get their financial affairs in order. The section on end-of-life preparation is detailed and precise. While all of the information is practical and financially based, it is the bringing together of psychological and spiritual issues that make it an unusual financial guide.

Pollan, Stephen, and Mark Levine.
Die Broke: A Radical Four-Part Financial Plan
New York: Harper Collins, 1997
While written by a trusted and successful financial advisor, the advice is unconventional and intriguing. The author suggests that: we do work that suits us, rather than that which will lead only to wealth; we use cash as much as possible, never going into debt except for a house or car; and we give away now the accrued wealth we have beyond our comfortable needs to those we love, while they need it and we can watch them enjoy it.

Sphinx Publishing, Legal Survival Guides
*How to Write Your Own Living Will, Living Trusts and Simple Ways to Avoid
   Probate,* and *The Power of Attorney Handbook*
Naperville, IL: Sourcebooks, Inc, 1998
Practical, do-it-yourself guidebooks for creating the above-named documents.

ORGANIZATIONS
AARP Legal Services Network
(800) 424-3410. *www.aarp.org/lsn*
Provides free consultation to association members. For attorneys in your area, look in your Yellow Pages under "Associations," "Attorneys" or "Lawyers" for the heading "AARP—Legal Services Network."

FUNERALS

BOOKS
Bennett, Amanda, and Terence B. Foley
In Memoriam: A Practical Guide to Planning a Memorial Service
New York: Simon & Schuster, 1997
Includes ideas for religious, secular, or creative services, both formal and informal. Chapters include verses to read, music from many categories, how to write a eulogy, and a checklist for the most practical needs to consider when a loved one has died.

McPhelimy, Lynn
In the Checklist of Life: A Working Book to Help You Live and Leave This Life!
Rockfall, CT: AAIP Publishing Co. LLC, 1997
Gives order to end-of-life facts and figures. There are spaces and instructions for lists of numbers, dates, things, locations, plans, and memories.

Poer, Nancy Jewel
Living Into Dying: A Journal of Spiritual and Practical Deathcare for Family and Community
Placerville, CA: White Feather Press, 2002
Poer's belief that death is a sacred passage illuminates this collection of personal stories, which come from years of helping families and communities care for their loved ones, before, during, and after death. Includes many aspects of deathcare, from spiritual guidance to instructions for building a casket.

Wiskind, Julie, and Richard Spiegel
Coming to Rest: A Guide to Caring for Our Own Dead
Kamuela, HI: Dovetail, Inc, 1998
If you are interested in providing personal care for your loved one's body after death without calling a mortician, this book will guide you. Simple and clear explanations of what you need to know from the time of death until the body has been either buried or cremated. Individual state requirements are also listed.

ORGANIZATIONS
Federal Trade Commission
Public Reference, Federal Trade Commission, Washington, D.C.
  20580
(202) 326-2222. w*ww.ftc.gov*
Write or call for pamphlet describing FTC's facts about funerals.

Final Passages
PO Box 1721, Sebastopol, CA 95473
(707) 824-0268. *www.finalpassages.org*
A model project offering education for personal and legal rights concerning home-and family-directed funerals and final disposition (burial and cremation). Their intention is to re-introduce the concept of funerals in the home as a part of family life and as a way to de-institutionalize death.

Funeral Consumers Alliance
33 Patchen Road, So. Burlington, VT 05403
(800) 765-0107. *www.funerals.org*
Lists the non-profit, volunteer-run organizations throughout the United States that make up the local societies that will help you receive the lowest funeral prices possible. The website will direct you to the organization closest to you and also contains answers to every possible question you could have regarding funerals.

Funeral Ethics Organization
PO Box 10, Hinesburg, VT 05461
(866) 866-5411. *www.funeralethics.org*
Their mission is to promote ethical standards in all death-related

transactions. This means working for better public understanding of the choices one has (and how to make them) concerning practitioners (funeral, cemetery, and the memorial trade industry), and public agencies (law enforcement and organ procurement organizations).

GRIEF

BOOKS
Buscaglia, PhD, Leo
The Fall of Freddie the Leaf: A Story of Life for All Ages
(See annotation under CHILDREN.)

Canfield, Jack, and Mark Victor Hansen
*Chicken Soup for the Grieving Soul: Stories About Life, Death, and
    the Loss of a Loved One*
Deerfield Beach, FL: Health Communications, Inc., 2003
This collection of stories shared by those who have lost a loved one provides comfort, peace, and understanding to those currently going through the process. Even though individuals deal with grief in their own ways and within their own time, guidance and support from others help ease the journey.

Childs-Oroz, PhD, Annette
Will You Dance?
Incline Village, NV: The Wandering Feather Press, 2002
Beautifully illustrated and poetically written, the author asks us to dance with change, fear, and loss. She reminds us that we will all be invited, and that the only way to arrive at peace and joy is to participate in the dance. An exquisite gift for anyone, but especially those who are faced with a current challenge of change, fear or loss.

Chodron, Pema
When Things Fall Apart: Heart Advice for Difficult Times
Boston and London: Shambala, 1997
Radical and compassionate advice for what to do when things fall apart in our lives—whether it be loss of a job, loss of a loved one, or a state of war. There is only one approach to suffering, says the author, and that is to

move toward painful situations with friendliness and curiosity. In the midst of chaos, we discover that love and truth are indestructible.

Elison, Jennifer, EdD, and Chris McGonigle, PhD
Liberating Losses: When Death Brings Relief
Cambridge, MA: Perseus Publishing, 2003
While most people who lose a loved one feel grief, some do not. The authors have gathered over forty stories, along with their own, of losses that led to relief. These provide a forum for many who have felt it unacceptable to express such nontraditional responses.

Han, Carolyn Everett
Kalapana
(See annotation under CHILDREN.)

Knapp, Ronald, J.
Beyond Endurance: When a Child Dies
New York
(See annotation under CHILDREN.)

Mundy, Michaelene
Sad Isn't Bad: A Good-Grief Guidebook for Kids Dealing with Loss
Illustrated by R.W. Alley
(See annotation under CHILDREN.)

Noel, Brook, and Pamela D. Blair, PhD
*I Wasn't Ready to Say Goodbye: Surviving, Coping, and Healing After
  the Sudden Death of a Loved One*
Fredonia WI: Champion Press Ltd., 2003.
From TWA Flight 800 to Columbine to 9/11, as well as fatal accidents in one's own neighborhood, the shock of sudden death adds another dimension to the grief felt after any loss. There is no time to prepare and no opportunity to say good-bye. Both the authors survived the unexpected death of a loved one and at the time could not find written material to help them cope. They tell the stories of interviewed survivors as well their own experiences.

ORGANIZATIONS
Compassionate Friends
PO Box 3696, Oak Brook, IL 60522
(877) 969-0010. *www.compassionatefriends.org*
Their mission is to assist families toward the positive resolution of grief following the death of a child of any age, and to provide information and support. It is a nonprofit, self-help support organization that offers friendship and understanding to bereaved parents, grandparents and siblings. There is no religious affiliation and there are no membership dues or fees.

Our House
West Los Angeles: 1950 Sawtelle Blvd. Suite 255, Los Angeles, CA 90025. (310) 475-0299. San Fernando Valley: 22801 Ventura Blvd. Suite 112, Woodland Hills, CA 91364 (818) 222-3392. *www.ourhouse-grief.org*
Provides the Los Angeles community with grief support services, education, resources and hope. Bereavement groups are offered for specific ages and types of loss.

HOSPICE (see PALLIATIVE CARE & HOSPICE)

LESSONS FOR LIVING FROM ILLNESS AND DYING

BOOKS
Bolen, MD, Jean Shinoda
Close to the Bone: Life-Threatening Illness and the Search for Meaning
New York: Scribner, 1996
Bolen uses myths, personal experience, and the stories of her patients and friends to guide those with life-threatening illness to a life-affirming state. She shows how serious illness helps us understand the preciousness of life by stripping away insignificant concerns.

Cobb, Nancy
In Lieu of Flowers: A Conversation for the Living
New York: Random House, 2000

In beautiful prose, the author describes her feelings and reflections over the death of both of her parents, a special friend, and others. Her loss of loved ones through Alzheimer's, suicide, and cancer helps the reader face his own feelings, speak the truth, and see death as an integral part of life.

Kübler-Ross, Elisabeth, MD, and David Kessler
*Life Lessons: Two Experts on Death and Dying Teach us About the Mysteries of
    Life and Living*
New York: Scribner, 2000
Each chapter describes a particular lesson learned during the care of dying patients, as well as Kübler-Ross' experiences since her own stroke.

Levine, Stephen
A Year to Live: How to Live this Year as if it Were Your Last
(See annotation under BUDDHIST PERSPECTIVES.)

Murphy, MD, N. Michael
The Wisdom of Dying: Practices for Living
Boston: Element Books, 1999
The author interweaves the intensely moving stories of those who have met death and those who have accompanied them with stories from ancient myth and legend. Insights gained from the author's decades of experience in guiding others on their journeys toward death may well change your approach to life.

Remen, MD, Rachel Naomi
Kitchen Table Wisdom: Stories that Heal
New York: Penguin Putnam, 1994
While this book is truly about living well, Remen's stories of people undergoing terminal illness help illuminate the process of growth and awareness that often comes at the end of life. There are almost 80 mini-chapters; each one may evoke tears of sadness and joy, and most often, of astonishment at the courage and strength of the human heart.

Remen's training, as well as her own chronic illness, give her perceptions both authority and compassion. Her simple, yet profound, way of describing these vignettes make it a must-read for everyone interested in life, death, illness, healing.

MEDICAL CHOICES

BOOKS
Callahan, Daniel
The Troubled Dream of Life: In Search of a Peaceful Death
Washington, DC: Georgetown University Press, 2000
(See annotation under BIOETHICS.)

_____. *Setting Limits: Medical Goals in an Aging Society*
Washington, DC: Georgetown University Press, 1987 and 1995
(See annotation under BIOETHICS.)

Dunn, Chaplain Hank
Hard Choices for Loving People: CPR, Artificial Feeding, Comfort Measures Only and the Elderly Patient
Herndon, VA: A & A Publishers, 2001
"This booklet is written to provide guidance to patients and their families who must face the 'hard choices' as they receive and participate in health care."

Nuland, MD, Sherwin B.
How We Die: Reflections on Life's Final Chapter
(See annotation under DYING PROCESS.)

ORGANIZATIONS
Consumer Health Information Program and Services (CHIPS)
151 East Carson Street, Carson, CA 90745
(310) 830-0909
This information and research gem is part of Los Angeles County Public Library. Simply tell the friendly personnel your health topic and questions, and in a few days the results of their in-depth research arrive in the mail. (They charge a nominal fee for the cost of copying.)

People's Medical Society
www.peoplesmed.org
America's largest nonprofit consumer health advocacy organization is dedicated to bringing information that will help you become a more informed and empowered medical consumer. From guarding your health

to guarding your hard-earned money, the books and other publications you'll find in the Health Library Catalog are designed for you—the medical consumer.

ORGAN AND TISSUE TRANSPLANTS

BOOKS
Caplan, Arthur, and Daniel H. Coelho
The Ethics of Organ Transplants: The Current Debate
Amherst, NY: Prometheus Books, 1998
A renowned bioethicist and a medical writer selected 34 articles (mostly recent) from the most important, influential, and up-to-date leaders in ethics, medicine, philosophy, law, and politics. They examine the numerous and tangled issues surrounding organ procurement and distribution: the search for new sources of organs; new methods of procurement; new ways of managing dying; and innovative strategies for fairly distributing this scarce life-saving resource. The bibliography includes web sites. No index.

Pearsall, PhD, Paul
The Heart's Code: Tapping the Wisdom and Power of Our Heart's Energy
New York: Random House, 1998
Pearsall, a psychoneuroimmunologist and best-selling author, gives "a fascinating synthesis of ancient wisdom, modern medicine, scientific research, and personal experiences that proves that the human heart, not the brain, hold the secrets that link body, mind, and spirit." His theory of "energy cardiology," amazing anecdotes and scientific data, and new findings about cellular memories form the basis for "tapping the wisdom and power of our heart energy." His stories were gathered from patients, including himself, who received organ transplants.

Sylvia, Claire, with William Novak
A Change of Heart: A Memoir
New York: Warner Books, 1998
"After a heart and lung transplant operation, dancer Claire Sylvia discovered that new organs were not the only thing she inherited. Never having liked such foods as beer and chicken nuggets, she suddenly started craving them. After an extraordinary dream, she seeks out the family of her

donor—a teenaged boy who died in a motorcycle accident—and learns that it is indeed possible for two souls to merge in one body."

ORGANIZATIONS
American Red Cross
2025 E Street NW, Washington, DC 20006
(202) 303-4498. *www.redcross.org*
With tissue donation, one donor can benefit as many as fifty people. For example, donated tissue is used for burn patients and certain sizes of heart valves. You must sign a donor card or note your wish on your driver's license; then also be sure to tell your family of your wish to donate tissue since they need to give consent. The Red Cross handles only tissue (not organ) donations.

Health Resources and Services Administration (HRSA)
US Dept. of Health and Human Services
Parklawn Building, 5600 Fisher Lane, Rockville, MD 20857
www.ask.hrsa.gov
Each day about sixty-three people receive an organ transplant, while another sixteen on the waiting list die because not enough donors are available. Download a donor card from this website. Share your decision with your family.

PALLIATIVE CARE & HOSPICE

BOOKS
Byock, MD, Ira
Dying Well: The Prospect for Growth at the End of Life
New York: Riverhead Books, 1997
A hospice doctor describes how patients and their loved ones can grow and change by participating consciously in the dying process, and how physical suffering can be alleviated. Actual patients' stories show the different aspects of how we may learn and live during this time. Byock is an active spokesperson about the availability and service of hospice and palliative care in the United States.

Callahan, Maggie, and Patricia Kelly
Final Gifts: Understanding the Special Awareness, Needs, and
   Communications of the Dying
New York: Bantam Books, 1992
Actual stories by two compassionate hospice nurses in which they illustrate
"near death awareness," the qualities and conditions patients display when
they are approaching death. If you are new to the hospice concept read this
book first. It is concise, moving and clear, and will likely draw you toward
wanting to know even more about hospice care.

De Hennezel, Marie
Intimate Death: How the Dying Teach Us to Live
Translated by Carol Brown Janeway
New York: Alfred E. Knopf, 1997
De Hennezel is a psychologist who became head of the first palliative care
unit in a Paris hospital for people with terminal illness. Her stories describe
how to talk to anyone who is dying, how to enrich our lives, and how to
bring back both peace and dignity to death.

Lattanzi-Licht, Marcia, with John J. Mahoney, and W. Galen Miller *The*
Hospice Choice: In Pursuit of a Peaceful Death
New York: A Fireside Book, 1998
The National Hospice Guide to hospice care is a must for learning all of
the different aspects of hospice; what it is, how to receive services, how to
give services. Stories are told and followed with specific information of a
practical nature. Contains an excellent resource guide of organizations,
websites and statistics related to hospice care.

Stoddard, Sandol
The Hospice Movement: A Better Way of Caring for the Dying New York:
Random House, 1992
First published in 1978 and updated in 1991, the history of the hospice
movement in the United States is chronicled and illustrated with
experiences told by hospice caregivers.

ORGANIZATIONS
American Academy of Hospice and Palliative Medicine
4700 W. Lake Avenue, Glenview, IL 60025

(847) 375-4712. *www.aahpm.org*
Dedicated to excellence in palliative medicine, the prevention and relief of
suffering among patients and their families, and fostering research.

Hospice Association of America
228 Seventh Street SE, Washington, DC 20003
(202) 546-4759. *www.hospice-america.org*
Includes 2,800 hospices and thousands of caregivers and volunteers.
Recently ranked the most effective health care trade organization on
Capitol Hill, it is the largest lobbying group for hospice.

National Hospice and Palliative Care Organization
1700 Diagonal Road, Alexandria, VA 22314
(703) 837-1500. *www.nhpco.org*
The vision of the organization is to create an America where every
individual can value the experience at end of life. The mission is to
advance the art and science of end-of-life care.

PERSONAL STORIES

BOOKS
Albom, Mitch
*Tuesdays with Morrie: An Old Man, a Young Man, and Life's
Greatest Lesson*
New York: Bantam Doubleday Dell, 1997
A former student spends a year of Tuesdays with his wise and kind
professor, Morrie Schwarz. Morrie is dying and is determined to stay
conscious until the end. As he lives through these months, he
communicates his life story, the wisdom he has gained, the vulnerability he
now feels as his body deteriorates, and how he continues to enjoy his
visitors, his wife, and his life. It is understandable why this book remained
on the best-seller list for well over three years.

Amole, Gene
The Last Chapter: Gene Amole on Dying
Denver, CO: Rocky Mountain News, 2002

For the last six months of his life, columnist for the Rocky Mountain News, Gene Amole, decided to write about his experience and share it with his readers. With humor and compassion, he describes the insights, which came with his increasing infirmity, and the richness of his final days.

Bernadin, Cardinal Joseph
The Gift of Peace: Personal Reflections
Chicago: Loyola Press, 1997
An exquisite memoir written by a Chicago Cardinal, during the final two months of his life, as he was dying. "The past three years have taught me a great deal about myself and my relationship to God, the Church, and others....Within these major events lies the story of my life—what I have believed and who I have worked hard to be. And because of the nature of these events, I have deepened and developed my own spirituality and gained insights that I want to share...."

Kübler-Ross, Elisabeth
The Wheel of Life: A Memoir of Living and Dying
New York: Touchstone, 1997
"Now, at age seventy-one facing her own death, this world-renowned healer tells the story of her extraordinary life. Having taught the world how to die well, she now offers a lesson on how to live well. Her story is an adventure of the heart—powerful, controversial, inspirational—a fitting legacy of a powerful life."

Nearing, Helen
Loving and Leaving the Good Life
White River Junction, VT: 1992
After living and writing about the "Good Life" for over 50 years, Helen Nearing compassionately describes the peaceful death of her husband Scott as he neared 100 years of age. She also describes her personal thoughts about aging and dying.

Sharp, Joseph
Living Our Dying: A Way to the Sacred in Everyday Life
New York: Hyperion, 1996
A long-term survivor of AIDS, the author shares his own experiences as well as those lives he has counseled as a chaplain and "conscious dying

advocate." He encourages the reader to maintain a sensitive awareness that our time on earth is indeed limited and that repressing thoughts of death makes living less vital.

Siegel, Joel
Lessons for Dylan: From Father to Son
New York: Public Affairs Press, 2003
Film critic Joel Siegel writes a memoir for his son, in case he doesn't have the opportunity to know him. Three cancer surgeries, chemotherapy, and radiation—during the year of his son's birth—caused him to consider the possibility that he could not tell these stories in person. (At this writing he is doing well and enjoying his time with Dylan.)

Warner, Gale
Dancing at the Edge of Life
New York: Hyperion, 1998
Gale Warner's passion for life and her talented ability to describe it to us makes this journal of her last 13 months a powerful and inspiring book. Between the arduous medical treatments for lymphoma, Gale continues to enjoy her days, her family, and friends. She articulates, in her poet's voice, what she is feeling physically, emotionally, and spiritually as she dances at the edge of life.

PURPOSE IN LIFE

BOOKS
Adrienne, Carol
The Purpose of Your Life: Finding Your Place in the World Using Synchronicity, Intuition, and Uncommon Sense
New York: William Morrow and Company, 1998
The author hopes that "by bringing you the stories of real people, some inner knowing and recognition of your own path will be touched." Principles and techniques are presented to increase creativity, leading you toward your own purpose in life.

Chapman, Joyce
Live Your Dream: Discover and Achieve Your Life Purpose
North Hollywood, CA: Newcastle, 1990
"The purpose of this book is to assist you in actively being the person you want to be, and acquiring the tools and skills necessary to achieve your ultimate potential."

Frankl, Victor E.
Man's Search for Meaning
New York: Simon and Schuster, 1959
This widely read book has inspired many people around the world to seek meaning and understand suffering. Living in concentration camps during World War II caused Frankl to find reasons to live. He found that "the will to meaning" is the basic motivation for human life. He suggests we not only ask what we want from life, but also what does life want from us.

Giese, Jo
A Woman's Path
Photographs by Jill Johnston
New York: Golden Books, 1998
Beautifully composed interviews and photographs of women who have made unique career choices at various stages of life.

Hillman, James
The Soul's Code: In Search of Character and Calling
New York: Random House, 1996
Hillman's "acorn theory" proposes that each life is formed by a particular image, an image that is the essence of that life and calls it to its destiny, just as the mighty oak's destiny is written in the tiny acorn. His theory offers a liberating vision of childhood troubles and an exciting approach to themes such as fate and fatalism, character and desire, family influence and freedom, and, most of all, calling. He asks us to address the invisible mystery at the center of every life, "What is it, in my heart that I must do, be, and have? And why?"

Marks, Linda
Living with Vision: Reclaiming the Power of the Heart
Indianapolis, IN: Knowledge Systems, 1989

"This book is intended to show that a sustainable future can be created, that each of us can make a difference, and each of us can make a mark on the world by being who we truly are."

Moore, Thomas
Care of the Soul: A Guide for Cultivating Depth and Sacredness in Everyday Life
New York: HarperCollins, 1992
Thomas Moore, an ex-priest and practicing psychotherapist "offers a new way of thinking about daily life—its problems and its creative opportunities. He proposes a therapeutic way of life that is not a self-improvement project. Instead, the focus is on looking more deeply into emotional problems and sensing sacredness in ordinary things."

OTHER MEDIA
Choquette, Sonia
Creating Your Heart's Desire (Audio tape, CD)
Niles, IL: Nightingale Conant, 1997
Lessons that will help you learn what you want out of life, eliminate obstacles, make decisions, and guard your dreams from self-doubt. Helpful guidelines in redirecting your purpose and dreams, especially in times of stress and impending change.

REINCARNATION

BOOKS
Cerminara, MD, Gina
Many Mansions: The Edgar Cayce Story on Reincarnation
New York: New American Library, 1978
Dr. Cerminara examines how the famed psychic penetrated the "previous lives" of his subjects and performed cures and prophecies that made him a notable clairvoyant.

Cranston, Sylvia, and Carey Williams
Reincarnation: A New Horizon in Science, Religion, and Society
New York: Crown Publishers, 1984
"This is the most comprehensive and effectively practical book ever

published on the subject of reincarnation. Bringing together the work of internationally reputable scientists, distinguished theologians, renowned social historians, and prominent psychologists, it presents the reader with the best that has been thought and written on this important area of human life."

Stevenson, MD, Ian
Cases Suggestive of Reincarnation
Charlottesville, VA: Praeger Publishing, 1980
Stevenson's thorough and compelling research has contributed to the popularity of the concept of reincarnation and its being taken seriously in the United States. His studies describe children who can recall details from lives with other families and in other locations. These are corroborated by visits and interviews. Also, current birth marks or defects are connected to accidents in former lives that led to death. Stevenson, who is Director of Personality Studies at the Health Sciences Center, University of Virginia, has been studying these cases for over forty years.

Weiss, MD, Brian
Many Lives, Many Masters
New York: Simon and Schuster, 1988
Psychiatry and metaphysics blend together in this fascinating book based on true case histories. As a graduate of Columbia and Yale Medical School and one who was once firmly entrenched in a clinical approach to psychiatry, Weiss found himself reluctantly drawn into past-life therapy when a hypnotized patient revealed surprising details of her past lives.

SPIRITUAL ISSUES

BOOKS (See also BOOKS under AFTERLIFE and BUDDHIST PERSPECTIVES.)

Elliott, William
Tying Rocks to Clouds: Meetings and Conversations with Wise and Spiritual People
New York: Doubleday, 1996
"With intrepid good spirits, author Bill Elliot interviews the world's foremost spiritual figures, acquainting us with their exuberant earthly charms, as well as their insight and intelligence. Propelled since childhood by the untimely deaths of his parents, Elliot traveled the globe to meet with these luminaries and directly find out their answers to the fundamental questions of existence: What is life's purpose? What is God or Ultimate Reality? Why do people suffer? Does a part of us live on after death?"

Participants include Robert Schuller, the Dalai Lama, Ram Dass, Mother Teresa, and B.F. Skinner, among many other notables.

Kramer, PhD, Kenneth
The Sacred Art of Dying: How World Religions Understand Death
Mahwah, NJ: Paulist Press, 1988
This book focuses primarily on religious attitudes toward death, dying, and afterlife, including Hindu, Buddhist, Zen, Tibetan, Chinese, Mesopotamian, Egyptian, Greek, Hebraic, Christian, Islamic and American Indian views. Kramer is an Associate Professor in the religious Studies Department at San Jose University in California.

Appendix III

Alphabetical Bibliography

For Books, Organizations and Other Media

BOOKS

Adrienne, Carol. *The Purpose of Your Life: Finding Your Place in the World Using Synchronicity, Intuition, and Uncommon Sense.* New York: William Morrow and Company, 1998.

Albom, Mitch. *Tuesdays with Morrie: An Old Man, a Young Man, and Life's Greatest Lesson.* New York: Bantam Doubleday Dell, 1997.

Amole, Gene. *The Last Chapter: Gene Amole on Dying.* Denver, CO: Rocky Mountain News, 2002.

Anaya, Rudolfo A. *Bless Me Ultima.* Berkeley, CA: TQS Publications, 1972.

Becker, Ernest. *The Denial of Death.* New York: Simon & Schuster, 1973.

Bennett, Amanda, and Terence B. Foley. *In Memoriam: A Practical Guide to Planning a Memorial Service.* New York: Simon & Schuster, 1997.

Bernadin, Joseph Cardinal. *The Gift of Peace: Personal Reflections.* Chicago: Loyola Press, 1997.

Bolen, MD, Jean Shinoda. *Close to the Bone: Life-Threatening Illness and the*

Search for Meaning. New York: Scribner, 1996.

Buscaglia, PhD, Leo. *The Fall of Freddie the Leaf: A Story of Life for All Ages.* Thorofare, NJ: Slack Incorporated, 1982.

Byock, MD, Ira. *Dying Well: The Prospect for Growth at the End of Life.* New York: Riverhead Books, 1997.

Callahan, Daniel. *Setting Limits: Medical Goals in an Aging Society.* Washington, DC: Georgetown University Press, 1987 and 1995.

____. *The Troubled Dream of Life: In Search of a Peaceful Death.* Washington, DC: Georgetown University Press, 2000.

Callahan, Maggie, and Patricia Kelly. *Final Gifts: Understanding the Special Awareness, Needs, and Communications of the Dying.* New York: Bantam Books, 1992.

Cameron, Julia. *The Artist's Way.* New York: Jeremy P. Tarcher, 1992.

Canfield, Jack, and Mark Victor Hansen. *Chicken Soup for the Grieving Soul: Stories About Life, Death, and Overcoming the Loss of a Loved One.* Deerfield Beach, FL: Health Communications, Inc., 2003.

Caplan, Arthur. *Am I My Brother's Keeper?: The Ethical Frontiers of Biomedicine.* Indiana University Press, 1998.

____. and Daniel Coelho. *The Ethics of Organ Transplants: The Current Debate.* Amherst, NY: Prometheus Books, 1998.

Capossela, Cappy, and Sheila Warnock. *Share the Care: How to Organize a Group to Care for Someone Who Is Seriously Ill.* New York: Simon & Schuster, 1995.

Carter, Jimmy. *The Virtues of Aging.* New York: Ballantine, 2000.

Cerminara, MD, Gina. *Many Mansions: The Edgar Cayce Story on Reincarnation.* New York: New America Library, 1978.

Chapman, Joyce. *Live Your Dream: Discover and Achieve Your Life Purpose.* North Hollywood, CA: Newcastle, 1990.

Childs-Oroz, PhD, Annette. *Will You Dance?* Incline Village, NV: The Wandering Feather Press, 2002.

Chodron, Pema. *When Things Fall Apart: Heart Advice for Difficult Times.* Boston and London: Shambala, 1997.

Cobb, Nancy. *In Lieu of Flowers: A Conversation for the Living.* New York: Random House, 2000.

Coelho, Paulo. *Veronika Decides to Die.* New York: HarperCollins, 1998.

Cranston, Sylvia, and Carey Williams. *Reincarnation: A New Horizon in Science, Religion, and Society.* New York: Crown Publishers, 1984.

Dalai Lama, His Holiness the. *Advice on Dying and Living a Better Life.* Translated and edited by Jeffrey Hopkins, PhD. New York: Atria Books, 2002.

____. *The Joy of Living and Dying in Peace.* San Francisco: HarperCollins, 1997.

Diamant, Anita. *The Red Tent.* New York: Picador USA, 1997.

Darling, David. *Soul Search: A Scientist Explores the Afterlife.* New York: Villard Books, 1995.

De Hennezel, Marie. *Intimate Death: How the Dying Teach Us to Live.* Translated by Carol Brown Janeway. New York: Alfred A. Knopf, 1997.

Dworski, Susan. *The Invisible Vazimba: A Madagascar Novel.* Venice, CA: Porcellana Press, 2001.

Elison, Jennifer, EdD, and Chris McGonigle. *Liberating Losses: When Death Brings Relief.* Cambridge, MA: Perseus Publishing, 2003.

Elliott, William. *Tying Rocks to Clouds: Meetings and Conversations with Wise and Spiritual People.* New York: Doubleday, 1996.

Frankl, *Victor E. Man's Search for Meaning.* New York: Simon and Schuster, 1959.

Gentry, F. Bruce and Jens C. Appel III. *The Complete Will Kit.* New York: John Wiley & Sons, 1997.

Giese, Jo. *A Woman's Path.* Photographs by Jill Johnston. New York: Golden Books, 1998.

Han, Carolyn Everett. *Kalapana.* Honolulu, HI: Island Heritage Publishing, 1999.

Hanson, Warren. *The Next Place.* Minneapolis, MN: Waldman House Press, 1997.

Hatch, Judge David Patterson (channeled through Elsa Barker). *Letters from the Light: An Afterlife Journal from the Self-Lighted World.* Originally published in 1914. Edited by Kathy Hart. Oregon: Beyond Words Publishing, 1997.

Hedtke, Lorraine. *Re-Membering Lives: Conversations with the Dying and Bereaved.* Amityville, NY: Baywood Publishing, 2004.

Hillman, James. *The Soul's Code: In Search of Character and Calling.* New York: Random House, 1996.

____. *The Force of Character and the Lasting Life.* New York: Ballantine, 1999.

Humphrey, Derek. *Final Exit.* New York: Dell, 1992.

Ilardo, Joseph A. *As Parents Age: A Psychological and Practical Guide.* Acton, MA: VanderWyk & Burnham, 1998.

____. and Carole R. Rothman. *Are Your Parents Driving you Crazy?: How to Resolve the Most Common Dilemmas with Aging Parents.* Acton, MA: VanderWyk & Burnham, 2001.

Jones, Constance. R.I.P.: *The Complete Book of Death and Dying.* New York: HarperCollins, 1997.

Knapp, Ronald, J. *Beyond Endurance: When a Child Dies.* New York: Schocken Books, 1986.

Kessler, David. *The Rights of the Dying.* New York: Harper Collins, 1997.

Kothari, MD, Manu L., and Lope A. Mehta, MD. *Death: A New Perspective in the Phenomena of Disease and Dying.* London: Marion Boyars Publishers, 1986.

Kramer, PhD, Kenneth. *The Sacred Art of Dying: How World Religions Understand Death.* Mahwah, NJ: Paulist Press, 1988.

Kübler-Ross, MD, Elisabeth. *Death: The Final Stage of Growth.* New York: Simon & Schuster, 1975.

___. *On Death and Dying: What the Dying Have to Teach Doctors, Nurses, Clergy, and Their Own Families.* New York: Macmillan Publishing Company, 1969.

___. *The Wheel of Life: A Memoir of Living and Dying.* New York: Touchstone, 1995.

___. and David Kessler. *Life Lessons: Two Experts on Death and Dying Teach us About the Mysteries of Life and Living.* New York: Scribner, 2000.

Lattanzi-Licht, Marcia, with John J. Mahoney and Galen W. Miller. *The Hospice Choice: In Pursuit of a Peaceful Death.* New York: A Fireside Book, 1998.

Levine, Stephen. *A Year to Live: How to Live This Year as if it Were Your Last.* New York: Doubleday, 1997.

Longaker, Christine. *Facing Death and Finding Hope.* New York: Doubleday, 1997.

Lynch, Thomas. *The Undertaking: Life Studies From the Dismal Trade*. New York: W.W. Norton & Company, 1997.

Lynn, MD, Joanne, and Joan Harrold, MD. *Handbook for Mortals: Guidance for People Facing Serious Illness*. New York: Oxford University Press, 1999.

Marcell, Jacqueline. *Elder Rage—or—Take My Father…Please!: How to Survive Caring for Aging Parents*. Irvine, CA: Impressive Press, 2000.

Marks, Linda. *Living with Vision: Reclaiming the Power of the Heart*. Indianapolis, IN: Knowledge Systems, 1989.

McLeod, Beth Witrogen. *Caregiving: The Spiritual Journey of Love, Loss, and Renewal*. New York: John Wiley & Sons, 1999.

McPhelimy, Lynn. *In the Checklist of Life: A Working Book to Help You Live and Leave This Life!* Rockfall, CT: AAIP Publishing Co. LLC, 1997.

Metzger, Deena. *Entering the Ghost River: Meditations on the Theory and Practice of Healing*. Topanga, CA: Hand to Hand Press, 2003.

Miller, PhD, Sukie. *After Death: How People Around the World Map the Journey After Life*. New York: Simon & Schuster, 1997.

Moody, Jr., MD, Raymond A. *Life After Life*. New York: Bantam Books, 1988.

Moore, Thomas. *Care of the Soul: A Guide for Cultivating Depth and Sacredness in Everyday Life*. New York: HarperCollins, 1992.

Mundy, Michaelene. *Sad Isn't Bad: A Good-Grief Guidebook for Kids Dealing with Loss*. Illustrated by R.W. Alley. St. Meinrad, IN: One Caring Place, Abbey Press, 1998.

Murphy, MD, N. Michael. *The Wisdom of Dying: Practices for Living*. Boston: Element Books, 1999.

Nearing, Helen. *Loving and Leaving the Good Life.* White River Junction, VT: 1992.

Noel, Brook, and Pamela D. Blair, PhD. *I Wasn't Ready to Say Goodbye: Surviving, Coping, and Healing After the Sudden Death of a Loved One.* Fredonia WI: Champion Press Ltd., 2003.

Nouwen, Henri J.M. *Our Greatest Gift: A Meditation on Dying and Caring.* New York: HarperCollins, 1994.

Nuland, MD, Sherwin B. *How We Die: Reflections on Life's Final Chapter.* New York: Random House, 1995.

Orman, Suze. *The 9 Steps to Financial Freedom: Spiritual Steps So You Can Stop Worrying.* New York: Crown Publishers, 1997.

Pearsall, PhD, Paul. *The Heart's Code: Tapping the Wisdom and Power of Our Heart's Energy.* New York: Random House, 1998.

Peck, MD, M. Scott. *In Heaven as on Earth: A Vision of the Afterlife.* New York: Hyperion, 1996.

___. *Denial of the Soul.* New York: Harmony Books, Crown Publishers, Inc., 1997.

Pipher, Mary. *Another Country: Navigating the Emotional Terrain of Our Elders.* New York: Penguin Putnam, 1999.

Poer, Nancy Jewel. *Living Into Dying: A Journal of Spiritual and Practical Deathcare for Family and Community.* Placerville, CA: White Feather Press, 2002.

Pollan, Stephen, and Mark Levine. *Die Broke: A Radical Four-Part Financial Plan.* New York: HarperCollins Publishers, 1997.

Quill, MD, Timothy E. *Death and Dignity: Making Choices and Taking Charge.* New York: W.W. Norton, 1993.

Quindlen, Anna. *One True Thing*. New York: Random House, 1994.

Ram Dass. *Still Here: Embracing Aging, Changing, and Dying*. New York: Penguin Putnam, 2000.

Remen, MD, Rachel Naomi. *Kitchen Table Wisdom: Stories That Heal*. New York: Penguin Putnam, 1994.

Rinpoche, Sogyal. *The Tibetan Book of Living and Dying*. San Francisco: Harper, 1994.

Rosenberg, Larry. *Living in the Light of Death: On the Art of Being Truly Alive*. Boston and London: Shambala, 2000.

Shaffer, Carolyn, and Kristin Anundsen. *Creating Community Anywhere: Finding Support and Connection in a Fragmented World*. New York: Jeremy P. Tarcher, 1993.

Sharp, Joseph. *Living Our Dying: A Way to the Sacred in Everyday Life*. NY: Hyperion, 1996.

Siegel, Joel. *Lessons for Dylan: From Father to Son*. New York: Public Affairs Press, 2003.

Stevenson, MD, Ian. *Cases Suggestive of Reincarnation*. Charlottesville, VA: Praeger Publishing, 1980.

Stoddard, Sandol. *The Hospice Movement: A Better Way of Caring for the Dying*. New York: Random House, 1992.

Sylvia, Claire. *A Change of Heart: A Memoir*. Boston: Little Brown, 1997.

Talamo, John. *Power of Attorney Handbook*. Naperville, IL: Sphinx Publishing, 2001.

Thich Nhat Hanh. *No Death, No Fear: Comforting Wisdom for Life*. New York: Riverhead Books, 2002.

Tobin, MD, Daniel R. *Peaceful Dying: The Step-by-Step Guide to Preserving Your Dignity, Your Choice, and Your Inner Peace at the End of Life.* New York: HarperCollins Publishers, 1999.

Tolstoy, Leo. "The Death of Ivan Ilych," *The Death of Ivan Ilych and Other Stories.* New York: Penguin Books, 1960.

Warda, Mark. *How to Make Your Own Will.* Naperville, IL: Sphinx Publishing, 2000.

Warner, Gale. *Dancing at the Edge of Life.* New York: Hyperion, 1998.

Waxman, Stephanie. *A Helping Handbook: When a Loved One is Critically Ill.* Los Angeles: Marco Press, 2000.

Webb, Marilyn. *The Good Death: The New American Search to Reshape the End of Life.* New York: Bantam Books, 1997.

Weiss, MD. Brian. *Many Lives, Many Masters.* New York: Simon and Schuster, 1988.

Wills-Brandon, Carla. *One last Hug Before I Go.* Deerfield Beach, FL: Health Communications, 2000.

Wiskind, Julie, and Richard Spiegel. *Coming to Rest: A Guide to Caring for Our Own Dead.* Kamuela, HI: Dovetail, Inc, 1998.

Zimmerman, Jack, and Virginia Coyle. *The Way of Council.* Las Vegas, NV: Bramble Books, 1996.

ORGANIZATIONS

AARP. 601 E Street NW, Washington, DC, 20049. (800) 424-3410. *www.aarp.org.* AARP Legal Services Network. *www.aarp.org/lsn*

AccentCare. (800) 834-3059. *www.accentcare.com*

Aging with Dignity. PO Box 1661, Tallahassee, FL 32302. (800) 562-1931. *www.agingwithdignity.org*

American Academy of Hospice and Palliative Medicine. 4700 W. Lake Avenue, Glenview, IL 60025. (847) 375-4712. *www.aahpm.org*

American Red Cross. 2025 E Street NW, Washington, DC 20006. (202) 303-4498. *www.redcross.org*

Americans for Better Care of the Dying. 4200 Wisconsin Avenue, 4th Floor, Washington, DC 20016. (202) 895-2660. *www.abcd-caring.org*

Association of Personal Historians. 870 NW 178th Avenue, Beaverton, OR 97006. (503) 645-0616. *www.personalhistorians.org*

California Partnership for Long-Term Care. Mail Stop 4100, PO Box 942732, Sacramento, CA 94234. (800) 227-3445. *www.dhs.ca.gov/cpltc*

Capitol Advantage. 2751 Prosperity Avenue, Suite 600, Fairfax, VA 22031. (800) 659-8708. *www.capwiz.com*

CareGuide. 12301 NW 39th St. Coral Springs, FL 33065. (888) 389-8839. *www.careguide.com*

Center for Living Council: The Ojai Foundation. 9739 Ojai-Santa Paula Road, Ojai, CA 93023. (805) 646-8343. *www.ojaifoundation.org*

Chalice of Repose Project, Inc. PO Box 169, Mt. Angel, OR 97362. *www.music-thanatologyassociation.com*

Choice in Dying. 200 Varick Street, 10th Floor, NY, NY 10014. (800) 989-9455. *www.choiceindying.org*

Cohousing Association of the United States. 1504 Franklin Street, Suite 102, Oakland, CA 94612. (510) 844-0865. *www.cohousing.org*

Compassionate Friends. PO Box 3696, Oak Brook, IL 60522. (877) 969-0010. *www.compassionatefriends.org*

Consumer Health Information Program and Services (CHIPS). 151 East Carson Street, Carson, CA 90745. (310) 830-0909.

Eden Alternative. Summerhill Company, 742 Turnpike Road, Sherburne, NY 13460. (607) 674-5232. *www.edenalt.com*

ElderWeb. 1305 Chadwick Drive, Normal, IL 61761. (309) 451-3319. *www.elderweb.com*

End-of-Life Choices. (Formerly *The Hemlock Society.*) PO Box 101810, Denver, CO 80250. (800) 247-7421. *www.endoflifechoices.org*

Ernest Becker Foundation. 3621 72nd Street, Mercer Island, WA 98040.

Federal Trade Commission. Public Reference, Federal Trade Commission, Washington, DC, 20580. (202) 326-2222. *www.ftc.gov*

Final Passages. PO Box 1721, Sebastopol, CA 95473. (707) 824-0268. *www.finalpassages.org*

Funeral Consumers Alliance. 33 Patchen Road, So. Burlington, VT 05403. (800) 765-0107. *www.funerals.org*

Funeral Ethics Organization. PO Box 10, Hinesburg, VT 05461. (866) 866-5411. *www.funeralethics.org*

Health Resources and Services Administration (HRSA). US Deptartment of Health and Human Services, Parklawn Building, 5600 Fisher Lane, Rockville, MD 20857. *www.ask.hrsa.gov*

Hemlock Society. (See *End-of-Life Choices.*)

Hospice Association of America. 228 Seventh Street SE, Washington, DC 20003. (202) 546-4759. *www.hospice-america.org*

L'Arche USA. (503) 282-6231. *www.larcheusa.org*

Last Acts Partnership: Advocating Quality End-of-Life Care (formerly called

Partnership for Caring and *Last Acts.)* 1620 Eye Street NW, Suite 202, Washington, DC 20006. (800) 989-9455. *www.lastacts.org*

Life Line. (800) 543-3546. *www.lifelinesys.com*

Medic Alert. 2323 Colorado Avenue, Turlock, CA 95302. (888) 633-4298.

National Hospice and Palliative Care Organization. 1700 Diagonal Road, Alexandria, VA 22314. (703) 837-1500. *www.nhpco.org*

National Association for Home Care. 228 7th St. SE, Washington, DC, 20003. (202) 547-7424. *www.nahc.org*

National Reference Center for Bioethical Literature. Kennedy Institute of Ethics, Georgetown University, PO Box 571212, Washington, DC 20057. (800) 246-3849. *www.bioethics.georgetown.edu*

National Shared Housing Resource Center. Rita Zadoff, 5342 Tilly Mill Road, Dunwoody, CA 30338. (770) 395-2625. *www.nationalsharedhousing.org*

Nursing Ethics Network (NEN). *www.nursingethicsnetwork.org*

Our House.
West Los Angeles: 1950 Sawtelle Blvd. Suite 255, Los Angeles, CA 90025. (310) 475-0299.
San Fernando Valley: 22801 Ventura Blvd., Suite 112, Woodland Hills, CA 91364. (818) 222-3344. *www.ourhouse.org*

Partnership for Caring. (800) 989-9455. (See *Last Acts Partnership.*)

People's Medical Society. *www.peoplesmed.org*

Rallying Points. 6620 Eye Street, Suite 202, Washington, DC 20006. (800) 341-0050. *www.rallyingpoints.org*

Sounds True. 413 S. Arthur Avenue, Louisville, CO 80306. (800) 333-9185, *www.soundstrue.com*

Toastmasters International. PO Box 9052, Mission Viejo, CA 92690. (949) 858-8255. *www.toastmasters.org*

Upaya Zen Center. 1404 Cerro Gordo, Santa Fe, NM 87501. (505) 986-8518. *www.upaya.org*

US Living Will. PO Box 2789, Westfield, NJ 07091. (800) 548-9455. *www.uslivingwillregistry.com*

Wellness Community—National. 10921 Reed Hartman Highway, Suite 215, Cincinnati, OH 45242. (888) 793-9355. *www.thewellnesscommunity.org*

World University of America Ojai. 1444 PO Box 1567, Ojai, CA 93024. (805) 646-1444. *www.worldu.edu*

OTHER MEDIA
(Booklets and pamphlets; audio tapes and CD; video and DVD)

And Thou Shalt Honor. (Video, DVD). *www.andthoushalthonor.com*

Creating Your Hearts's Desire. (Audio Tapes). Sonia Choquette. Niles, IL: Nightingale Conant, 1997.

Graceful Passages: A Companion for Living and Dying. (CD set with 56-page book). Companion Arts, PO Box 2528, Novato, CA 94948. (888) 242-6608. *www.wisdomoftheworld.com*

Hard Choices for Loving People: CPR, Artificial Feeding, Comfort Measures Only and the Elderly Patient. (Booklet) Dunn, Chaplain Hank. Herndon. VA: A & A Publishers, 1994.

On Our Own Terms: Moyers on Dying in America. (Video) *www.pbs.org/wnet/onourownterms/*

Sounds True. (Audiotapes and CDs). 413 S. Arthur Avenue, Louisville, CO 80306. (800) 333-9185. *www.soundstrue.com*

Who Will Speak for Robert? The Importance of Having an Advance Care Directive. (Video) Produced by Center for Humane and Ethical Medical Care (CHECK√), 1250 16th Street, Santa Monica, CA 90404. (310) 319-4189.

"Wit" Film Project. Contact Jennifer Spooner. (310) 478-3711, Ext. 48353. *www.growthhouse.org/witfilmproject/*

Appendix IV

Life Story Interview

CHILDHOOD

★   Where, when, and how did you grow up?
★   What did your dad do for work...your mom...what do you remember the most about them?
★   What do you remember about your grandparents?
★   Did you have brothers and sisters...what do you remember most about them?
★   What kind of child were you and what did you like to do?
★   What kind of school did you go to...what did you like at school...any favorite teachers or incidents you recall?
★   What did you want to be when you grew up?

ADOLESCENCE

★   What were you like as a teenager?
★   What was high school like for you?
★   Who were your best friends?
★   What was the hardest thing about growing up?
★   What did you like to do then?
★   Do you have any favorite memories or incidents?
★   Did you have any jobs or work that you did then?

ADULTHOOD

★   Did you go to college…when…where…what was it like?

★   What are your favorite memories or incidents of that time?

★   Who were your favorite friends then?

★   Were you in the military?

★   When…what did you do…where did you go…who were your best friends…what do you remember the most?

FAMILY

★   When did you first meet your husband/wife…what was it like…what do you remember the most…what did you like best about him/her…do you remember any favorite dates or things you used to do together?

★   What would you like him/her to remember the most about you?

★   What have you always liked the best about him/her?

★   What do you wish for him/her for the rest of his/her life?

★   What do you remember the most about each of your children…pregnancies and deliveries…what do you like the best in each one of them?

★   What were they like as children?

★   What is the most special thing about each of them to you?

★   What would you like to tell them to remember the rest of their lives?

★   How do you hope each of their lives turns out?

PERSONAL

★   What have you liked best about your life so far?

★   What about your work and your professions?

★   What is the most important thing that you have learned in your life?

★   What were the most difficult times in your life?

★   Were you able to resolve whatever happened then?

★   Is there anything you would like to talk about now that you have not spoken of before?

★ What has it been like for you to be ill…has it changed you…the way you look at life…at people?

★ What is it like to be dying…has it changed the way you look at life, friends, family?

★ How much longer would you like to live?

★ What would you like to accomplish?

★ What is most important about life?

SPIRITUAL

★ What spiritual beliefs guided you throughout your life?

★ How did they help you?

Created by John Hart and used by Roberta Kay, MFCC.

Index

About the Author

Laura Larsen is a graduate of the UCLA School of Nursing and the Santa Monica School of Massage. For almost two decades, she has been a practicing massage therapist and dance-exercise teacher. During the past six years, she has been leading Facing the Final Mystery Workshops, which provide accredited continuing education units for nurses, social workers, and psychotherapists.

Laura would be pleased to hear from you regarding any end-of-life experiences you have had, ways in which this book has proven to be helpful, as well as interest you have in hosting a Facing the Final Mystery Workshop, or inviting her to speak to your organization or your community.

Laura Larsen RN
PO Box 6192
Malibu, CA 90264
laura@lauralarsen.com
www.lauralarsen.com